Canonmill

And there are other sights and exploits which crowd back upon my mind under a very strong illumination of remembered pleasure. But the effect of not one of them all will compare with the discoverer's joy, and the sense of old Time and his slow changes on the face of this earth, with which I explored such corners as Canonmills or Water Lane, or the nugget of cottages at Broughton Market. They were more rural than the open country, and gave a greater impression of antiquity than the oldest land upon the High Street. They too, like Fergusson's butterfly, had a quaint air of having wandered far from their own place; they looked abashed and homely, with their gables and their creeping plants, their outside stairs and running mill-streams; there were corners that smelt like the end of the country garden where I spent my Aprils; and the people stood to gossip at their doors, as they might have done in Colinton or Cramond.

Robert Louis Stevenson, *Edinburgh: Picturesque Notes*

The Inverleith development depended
on the old bridge across the Water
of Leith at Canonmills.

A.J. Youngson, *The Making of Classical Edinburgh*

By despising all that has preceded us, we
teach others to despise ourselves.

William Hazlitt

To the ever-cheerful and
inspiring Abbeyfield 'family'
at 17 Inverleith Row

Photographs, unless otherwise stated, are by the author.

Canonmills
and
Inverleith

JOYCE M. WALLACE

JOHN DONALD PUBLISHERS LTD
EDINBURGH

ISBN 0 85976 400 1

British Library Cataloguing in Publication Data

A catalogue record for this book is available from the British Library.

Acknowledgements

The staff of the Edinburgh Room at Edinburgh Central Library
The Michael Laird Partnership
The Scottish Life Assurance Company
The Standard Life Assurance Company
Mrs M. Wilson, Headteacher, Canonmills School
Desmond Hodges Esq., Director, Edinburgh New Town Conservation
    Committee
The Scotsman Publications, Ltd.

I am particularly indebted to Mr John W.B. Caldwell, who
has kindly read the Canonmills typescript and made many
helpful suggestions, and who has also prepared the illustration
of the Baxters' lintel; and to Mr Alan P. Bennell of the Royal
Botanic Garden, Edinburgh, who has read the chapter concerning
the Garden and made a number of most helpful comments on the text.

Typeset by ROM-Data Corporation Ltd., Falmouth, Cornwall.
Printed in Great Britain by Bell & Bain Ltd., Glasgow.

Contents

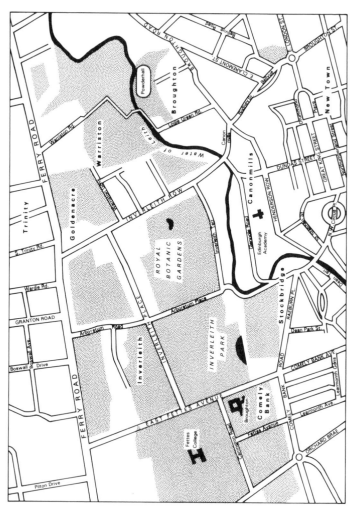

Present-day map of Canonmills and Inverleith.

CANONMILLS

CHAPTER 1

The Loch and the Mills

The area lying on the north side of Edinburgh and still known today as Canonmills is of very ancient origin. The village of that name was contained within the Barony of Broughton and was founded by the Augustinian canons who were brought to Holyrood by King David I who, in 1128, constructed his abbey church at the eastern end of the Royal Mile where the Old Town was confined on its ridge of rock until the extension of the royalties in the 1760s.

The monks came down to the banks of the 'Great River of the Water of Leith' to set up their mills, one being built for them by the king himself, between what later came to be known, from the tannery on the river-bank, as Tanfield and 'Puddocky' ('puddock' meaning frog), that stretch of the Water of Leith between Canonmills Bridge and St Mark's Farm. The farm is now built over but the old name survives in St Mark's Park and St Mark's Bridge across the Water, now a much reduced stream from its earlier days when it truly justified its description of a 'great river'. To these mills the Incorporation of Baxters, or Bakers, of the Canongate and the whole of the Barony of Broughton were 'thirled' (being compelled by law either to have their corn ground here or to pay a fine) as both the Canons' and Broughton

1

Mills were granted to Holyrood Abbey by King David in 1143. At the Reformation they became the property of the Logans of Restalrig who sold them to the Edinburgh Town Council in 1617, but in 1630 the lands of Broughton were purchased by Charles I. Being short of money, however, he disposed of them six years later to the Heriot Trust. The *History of St Cuthbert's* gives Canon Mylnes and Broughtoun as the 20th division of St Cuthbert's or West Kirk Parish in 1642.

A little to the south the waters of Canonmills Loch stretched originally, in a natural hollow, from what became the northern end of Dundas Street (formerly known as Pitt Street) eastwards to what is now Rodney Street, and northwards from the site of Royal Crescent to that of Eyre Place.

A number of lakes were formed, such as Duddingston and Lochend among those still extant in Edinburgh, at the end of the Ice Age about Ten thousand BC. Moving from west to east across the country the ice sheets or glaciers, carrying with them large, rough stones and rock fragments, carved out valleys in the softer rocks and deposited boulders of ice in natural or scooped-out hollows. These deposits melted and became sheets of water or natural lakes. Many of these lochs, Corstorphine being the largest in the Edinburgh area, were drained as far back as the seventeenth century. But glacial activity does not appear to have created the loch at Canonmills. In *Some Ancient Landmarks of Midlothian* Henry M. Cadell includes it in his map of *The Site of Edinburgh in Ancient Times*. It was, he says, 'a pool connected with the Water of Leith' which occupied the hollow overlooked (but not until that part of it had been drained) by Royal Crescent. 'It is', he continues, 'referred to in old maps and descriptions of Edinburgh and was not completely removed till 1865 when the last part of it was drained during the construction of the Royal Gymnasium'. It is possible that at some early period the Water of Leith, probably then a very substantial river, overflowed its banks to such an extent that it reached, and filled, the natural hollow, which then became the loch. It has been estimated that it was similar in size to Duddingston Loch (originally a much larger sheet of water) as it is at the present time.

An old raised beach stretched from this area eastwards across what is now the district of Bellevue where St Mary's Church, built in 1824, has its foundations in one of the Bellevue sand pits which are recorded in the town council minutes, and shells were found in the sandy soil on which Fettes Row and Royal Crescent were later built.

An attempt at drainage was made at Canonmills in the mid-eighteenth century which confined what was left of the loch to the north-east corner, the partially dried-up bed being then known as Canonmills Haugh.

Although no more than four feet deep, the loch attracted anglers to its banks to fish for perch, and fowlers with their guns which cracked and echoed across the placid lake as they targeted its ducks and waterfowl which were soon being carried homewards 'for the pot'. Coot and waterhen, woodcock and snipe built their nests in the sedges which lined its banks and a wheatfield lay to its immediate west.

The mills were on the south side of the river and gradually the villagers built up around them their little farms and cottages, their descendants witnessing such subsequent events of history as impinged on their otherwise quiet and rural lives. In 1544 they would see the Earl of Hertford's English army as it marched across the Wardie Muir from Granton, where it had landed, to the ford at 'Puddocky' where Cardinal Beaton had placed his artillery for the purpose of intercepting them with, according to an old English account, 'small effect and less resolution'. So they marched on to surprise Leith and 'plunder its richly laden dinner tables' before subjecting the port to fire and sword.

By 1571 the Frenchmen brought over by the Queen Regent, Mary of Guise, the mother of Mary Queen of

Scots, to help her against the Lords of the Congregation in the wars of the Reformation were riding out from Leith and 'parading recklessly before the town of Edinburgh' to display their bravery. But the Castle guns were turned towards them and a well-aimed volley scored a hit as they came to Broughton. It has been recorded that in 1642 an order was issued for the return of weapons which had been 'lent furthe of ye said tounis munitioun-house be ye said Provost, Bailes an Counsell... for ye publick and guid caus two yeiris syne and undeliverit bak again'. They were to be handed over to 'Alexr Willsoun of Canonmylins', or Canonmylnis as it was often written.

A late 17th-century diversion for the villagers was the hounding of Peter de Bruis, or de Braweis, who, with greater optimism than foresight, went into playing-card production and set up a paper mill by the Water of Leith at Canonmills. He even secured a monopoly for selling them which entitled him to 'search for and confiscate any contraband cards' and, as he exercised this right somewhat over-zealously, he brought down the ire and irritation of the natives upon his head. Jealousy of a foreigner's success aroused one Alexander Hunter to demolish his mills and, for good measure, to fling 'his unfortunate wife into the dam, using opprobrious words' as he did so. Hunter was fined fifty pounds for his pains and de Bruis then turned his attention to imported cards, bringing an action against Sir James Dick and Thomas Young who, he said, had infringed his rights. Although they had been brought in before his patent had been granted, the two importers were ordered 'to sell or otherwise dispose of them'. By this time de Bruis had had enough of 'local prejudice' and removed himself to Glasgow in 1683.

This versatile and undoubtedly skilled Dutchman (it is possible he may have been German) was active in other parts of the city as well as at Canonmills. Charles J.

Smith in *Historic South Edinburgh* calls him Peter Bruschi
but gives two German alternatives—Breusch and Brauss.
He mentions the Canonmills venture on which de Bruis
embarked after fulfilling a contract, in his capacity as an
engineer, between him and the Town Council to construct
'a leaden pipe of a three-inch bore, to be laid one foot
deep in the ground' for the purpose of conveying the
water of Comiston Springs to the newly-built reservoir at
the north-east end of the Castle Esplanade—the first
piped water supply to the city which was then wholly
confined to the southern side of the Nor' Loch. (This
reservoir, that part of it which is above ground having
been rebuilt in the nineteenth century, has been drained
of water and alternative uses are now under consideration). For this work de Bruis received a fee of £2,900
and a gratuity of a further £50 for carrying it out 'with
diligence and care'. As the 'springs were some two hundred feet higher than the . . . reservoir, it was possible
for the water to reach its destination at Castlehill by the
force of gravity'. This undertaking was completed in
1681. After his misfortunes at Canonmills Charles Smith
writes that, 'Undeterred, he opened another paper mill at
Restalrig and, in a different role, was appointed by James
VII as printer to the Royal Household in Holyrood,
where mob violence again forced him to flee. He is ac-
credited with being one of the first printers in Scotland
of playing cards.' It may have been as a consequence of
the mob violence that he fled to Glasgow. His first playing-card factory had been in Leith and John Russell in
The Story of Leith calls him Peter Bruce, an 'Ingeneer
German', who 'apparently thought it might pay better to
assume a Scottish name than to retain his own.'

He appears to have been a man of prodigious energy
and wide achievement. In a little volume by Will Grant,
F.S.A. Scot., written about 1950 on the Chapel and Castle of Rosslyn, he is found at work here also:

The Dutch contractor Peter Bruschi who brought the first public gravitation water supply to the City of Edinburgh from Tod's Well, Comiston, in 1676, brought water in lead pipes to the inner Court and lower Vaults of Rosslyn Castle in the time of Sir James St Clair, who . . . was responsible for obtaining Bruschi's services for the city.

New centuries breeding new ideas, around the year 1700 a rather grandiose proposal was made to make Edinburgh's river a navigable waterway 'whereby ships may pass and enter into the North Lough'. All that was needed, it was believed, was to make it deeper from the Bridge of Leith up to Inverleith and then 'cut through the Narrow Tract of Land from thence to the North Lough'. The great merit of this plan, it was argued, was that 'the mills of Canonmills and Boniton [Bonnington]' would not be affected by the undertaking. But although all this came to nothing, being a lot more easily said than done, the river continued to be a source of wealth to the millers. It was eventually not too much of an exaggeration to say, though it was of course 'said scathingly', that the Water of Leith had hardly any water running in it 'as most was drawn off into the lades'.

Cumberland Hill, in *Reminiscences of Stockbridge and Neighbourhood*, describes the occasion of the last riding of the Marches—or surveying of the boundaries—which took place in 1717 and was never again repeated. The village inhabitants would watch, impressed with the size and splendour of the spectacle, as the magistrates, town councillors and leading representatives from Leith and the neighbouring estates and farms, 'sumptously apparelled, mounted on stately horses and accompanied by a band of music', made their solemn and ceremonious way along the streets and then the country roads and paths in their circuitous journey. Leaving the old town, this 'long and pompous cavalcade' descended into the valley to the north and proceeded to their first destination, Canonmills. From there they went on to Stockbridge, across the Water of Leith to Dean, back by the river to Drumsheugh and then round to 'St Cuthbert's Churchtown'. From 'thence, wending eastwards along the northern side of the "Nordloch" to its eastern extremity', they returned to the auld toun which they entered by the West Port.

By the mid-eighteenth century Canonmills Loch had been drained from the area which lies today between Royal Crescent and Eyre Place, leaving a much smaller sheet of water at the north-eastern end in the angle defined by the Broughton Road end of Eyre Place and the ground to the west of Rodney Street. The main mill lade, running in wooden troughs and diverted from the Water of Leith upstream at the Dean Village (originally the

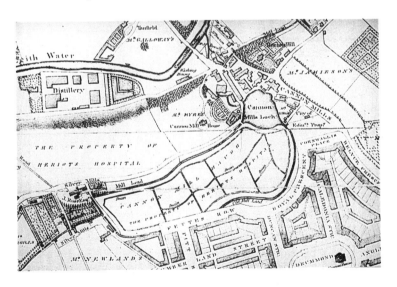

Detail from Ainslie's map of 1804 showing Canonmills Haugh, the remaining section of Canonmills Loch and Canonmills House.

Water of Leith Village), which also served Stockbridge and Silvermills, ran eastwards, after passing through these two villages, to the drained area shown on Ainslie's map of 1804 as Canon Mill Haugh. (This drained area, which now consisted of marsh and pasturage for cattle, is marked on some maps as 'Meadow' and on others as 'Canon Mill Haugh'.) Branching to the north and south sides of the Haugh, it then flowed into what remained of the loch, emerging as a single lade to turn the wheels at Canonmills and finally to rejoin the river at St Marks a short distance to the east of Canonmills Bridge.

Claiming to be older than the Duddingston Club which was founded in the closing years of the eighteenth century, Canonmills Curling Club made good use of the loch during the hard winters when the ice was 'bearing'. After the draining of the Nor' Loch in the northern valley below the old town, the curlers had moved to Canonmills, where they held an annual celebration prior to which they marched down the hill singing the 'Curlers' March' and accompanied by the magistrates and town councillors. The evening was spent in feasting and the drinking of ale and whisky. Such activities were brought to an end when the remaining part of the loch was drained in 1847.

One solitary and much-altered building, including the projection which housed the wheel, survives from the great days of milling at Canonmills but it only dates back to the late seventeenth or early eighteenth century and was converted in 1987 into six thousand square feet of open-plan office space. The ground floor at the Eyre Place corner had been used as shops from a much earlier date. At the top of Canon Street (where it joins Eyre Place) this four-storey mill building, now known as the Canon Mill, had successfully defied the demolition contractors since 1865 when those who followed the ancient trade at last abandoned the 'fast-flowing lade, slow grinding wheels and granaries to store the result of their

The Canon Mill in 1982 before restoration.

The Canon Mill after restoration.

labours'. The lade itself was still in use till nearer the end of the century. The oldest part of the village was here between Eyre Place and the Esso filling station at the foot of Canon Street. At the service station an old lintel inscribed in cursive writing *the Baxters land 1686* can still be seen a short distance across the forecourt where, rescued from the previous building at this point, it has been incorporated into the outside wall of its modern successor.

On the northern bank of the Haugh and to the immediate west of the diminished loch, on a site which was later occupied by the Davidson Memorial Church in Eyre Place, stood Canonmills House built in the early nineteenth century by James Eyre, a brewer from the Cowgate in the Old Town of Edinburgh from around the year 1780. Abutting the west side of the house was the main mill lade which changed direction several times before returning to the river. By 1810 he had come down to live beside the waters which he was now using for his lochside brewery, thus giving his name to the streets which were afterwards developed here and which still survive long after he himself has been forgotten. Earlier his name was also given as Eayr and Ayre. In 1832 his wife was living at No. 17 Dundas Street, so his death prob-

The old Baxters' land lintel built into a modern Garage wall at Canonmills
(Prepared and drawn from a rubbing by John W.B. Caldwell).

ably took place at or some time before that date. On a map prepared for the Post Office Directories later in the century the reduced loch is shown as 'Mill Pond' and the plain, symmetrical, two-storeyed house with its chimneys above its gable-ends as 'Eyre House', following the old Scottish custom of calling a house by the name of its owner. It has, however, been described as a 'fine mansion' with extensive gardens and grounds and, from a photograph showing the rear of the house and part of the garden, it would appear that some additions were made to the building from time to time. The map records Eyre Crescent curving deeply around and behind it in the days before the church was built.

After James Eyre's death the house and grounds were acquired by Patrick Neill, LL.D FRSE, who, says Lord Cockburn in *Memorials of His Time*, 'conducted a large printing business in Old Fishmarket Close' in the High Street of Edinburgh which had been established in 1749. His 'leisure was devoted to scientific and literary pursuits' and he was portrayed in the once-famous Chaldee Manuscript, written by, among others, John Gibson Lockhart, the son-in-law and biographer of Scott, as a 'lean man who hath his dwelling by the great pool to the north of the New City'. Before he removed to Canonmills House Dr Neill lived in Canonmills Cottage which, despite its name, was quite a substantial house situated behind the site on which the Ritz Cinema was later to be built when access was obtained by a lane at the side of the cinema. It was also visible from the foot of Scotland Street. Canonmills Cottage and its garden, over which much care and labour were expended, lay on land which sloped down to the loch, land which had been inherited by Neill himself and on which the printing works which will be referred to later were eventually built. Canonmills Cottage (or Canonmills Lodge as it is called on the Ordnance Survey map of 1896) was not swept away until the 1970s.

Patrick Neill (1776 - 1851), who later received the

honorary degree of LL.D from Edinburgh University, was the son of James Neill, a native of Haddington, who became apprenticed to James Cochrane, printer in Burnet's Close in the Old Town of Edinburgh, the firm which, in 1739, printed the first number of *The Scots Magazine*. Twenty years later they started a new newspaper called the *Edinburgh Chronicle* and the fact that no copies of it now exist may be due to their having been destroyed in the fire at the Rodney Street printing works in 1916. He became a partner in Hamilton & Balfour, later Hamilton, Balfour & Neill, printers to the Town and College, which, by 1766, was wholly owned by him. He removed to Old Fishmarket Close in 1769. Retiring in 1771, he bought the house and farm of Redpath in Berwickshire where he lived till his death in 1789 when his eldest son, Patrick, succeeded to the business and the Canonmills estate.

Canonmills House and Loch (from *Old and New Edinburgh* by James Grant)

Patrick took on William Fraser as his general manager and was now able to devote himself, beside the 'great pool', to the cultivation of rare and beautiful plants and flowers for which he was praised by Cockburn as a useful citizen, a most intelligent florist and author of the article *Gardening* in the *Encyclopaedia Britannica*. He was largely responsible for the founding of the Caledonian Horticultural Society in 1809 and for planning their Experimental Gardens at Inverleith. And he was also among those who were principally involved in the draining of the 'historic but nauseous Nor' Loch', going on thereafter to design West Princes Street Gardens where, in 1830, five acres were laid out as gardens and thousands of trees and shrubs were planted to his instructions. His interests extended to archaeology and the preservation of architectural relics and he was instrumental in saving the old tower in the Vennel, on the west side of Heriot's School, from demolition. He was also a member of St Mary's Parish Church.

Crombie included the 'lean' figure of Patrick Neill among his caricatures of contemporary *Modern Athenians*. He died unmarried in 1851 when the firm passed to William Fraser's sons, Alexander Fraser and Patrick Neill Fraser. In 1899 the business and the printing presses were removed to Rodney Street where, extending back to the Scotland Street railway line, they occupied about half an acre.

Canonmills House was pulled down in 1879 and the Gothic Revival Davidson Church (which had its origins in the Secession movement and whose congregation united with St Bernard's South to become St Bernard's-Davidson Church in 1945) was built in Eyre Place to fill the space left in the 'deep and opressive U', as *Buildings of Scotland: Edinburgh* expresses it, of Eyre Crescent. This little church, its tower topped by a pyramidal roof instead of the intended steeple, fell on evil days when it became a wholesale sweet-manufacturers' warehouse, and its

Eyre Place Church in 1971.

Flats built on the site of Eyre Place Church after its demolition in 1990.

crumbling walls were finally cast down in 1990 to be replaced by modern flats.

An old tradition asserts that Canonmills House was haunted by a lady who was said to sit in one of the windows. The locals were afraid to approach the house at night and the boys of the area are reputed to have called out to the ghost before taking to their heels!

Long before the reclamation of the Mill Pond, as the last remnant of the old loch had been called, in 1847, the northern extension of the New Town was being planned and built. By the end of the 1820s it had reached Fettes Row and Royal Crescent on the southern banks of the Haugh. 'The best thing about Royal Crescent', says *The Buildings of Scotland: Edinburgh*, 'is that it was built at all, and that the outward-looking perimeter of the Northern New Town was thus adequately, if not triumphantly, completed'. Planned, along with the rest of the Second New Town (as the area between the north side of Queen Street and Fettes Row/Royal Crescent was known) by Sir Robert Reid and William Sibbald, the plans were produced by the City Superintendent of Works, Thomas Brown. The Greek Doric doorways of this elegant Georgian crescent were only separated by the street itself, and by railings, from the lower level of the Haugh, and the waters of the loch had become only a distant memory by the time Eyre Place and Crescent were built, on what had been their opposite bank, on the estate of James Eyre in the late nineteenth century.

'The tunnel to the Scotland Street Station, the sight of the train shooting out of its dark maw with the two guards upon the brake, the thought of its length and the many ponderous edifices and open thoroughfares above, were certainly things of paramount impressiveness to a young mind'. So wrote Robert Louis Stevenson in *Edinburgh: Picturesque Notes* about the railway tunnel which, with its accompanying platforms, made an appearance at

Scotland Yard Adventure Playground showing one of the entrances for trains in the Scotland Street Tunnel.

the south-eastern end of the Haugh when the laying of the track had been completed. A.J. Youngson, in *The Making of Classical Edinburgh*, writes of the opposition with which proposals to route railway lines through Princes Street Gardens to the Waverley Station were met when they were first put forward. This criticism gradually abated, however, as a result of the early Victorian 'railway mania'. But another consideration also advantageous to the proposals 'was the existence of the Edinburgh, Leith and Newhaven Railway Company, incorporated in 1836, which opened a line from Scotland Street to Trinity in 1842 and which had plans to extend its line southwards to the site of the present Waverley Station'. These plans were carried out and the tunnel which so fascinated Stevenson was constructed in two parts so that two 'dark maws' faced each other, with the platforms in between, at the foot of Scotland Street and to the immediate west of the present Rodney Street. That this part of the line was, so to speak, above ground was quite deliberate. Not only did it enable passengers to board or leave the trains but it also provided a suitable place for carrying out certain procedures which brought curious spectators as well as potential passengers to Scotland Street Station. The tunnel, which ran from the long-vanished Canal Street (represented today by the carriageway at the Waverley Bridge entrance and so called from the proposed but never created canal in the Nor' Loch Valley) at the Waverley end, was very steep. It had a gradient of 1 in 27 and passed under St Andrew Square and Drummond Place on its way to Canonmills, and for this journey to be made at all it was necessary to control the downhill speed and give powerful assistance on the upward stretch. The southbound trains were coupled to a cable-hauling mechanism operated by a winding engine at Canal Street, while those going in the opposite direction were attached to break wagons to slow down their descent. The coupling and uncoupling operations took place at Scotland Street. Passengers were carried on this line for twenty years but maintenance costs were high and the locomotion methods cumbersome, with the result that the station became a goods yard used only for mineral traffic when the North British Railway Company took it over in 1862 and a new route to Trinity and Granton was opened via Leith Walk to avoid the tunnel which was closed in 1868. The 'dark maws' at Scotland Street were given over to mushroom growing in the 1920s but this was never very successful as a commercial enterprise. The northern end of the tunnel with its arched opening, where the trains on the seaward route emerged to complete their journey in daylight and fresh air, can still be seen near the top of Broughton Road.

The tunnel ran at a depth of seventy feet below the ground and was consequently used as an air raid shelter during the Second World War although, after one early air attack, very few later bombs were dropped in the Edinburgh area. Capable of accommodating as many as

One of the tickets issued to passengers on the Scotland Street to Trinity railway line.

three thousand people, it was primarily intended for the Waverley Station staff and an electric fan at the Waverley end provided ventilation. After the war the Canonmills section of the tunnel became a warehouse, for Cochrane's Garages, for cars newly off the production line. The track was reopened for one day on 31st August 1963 when a specially chartered train carried railway historians via Scotland Street down to Trinity. It is possible that the tunnel may be used for the proposed Edinburgh metro system should this ever be constructed.

A few years ago the Edinburgh New Town Conservation Committee in Dundas Street was given part of the station yard in which to store 'spare parts' (such as railings, balconies, columns, capitals and mouldings) for use in the repair of flats and houses in the New Town. This interesting 'Alladin's Cave' has now been closed, however, but the Edinburgh Architectural Salvage Yard in Leith provides a similar service.

Referring to the meadow and marshland on the Haugh, James Grant writes, 'In this quarter we now find the Patent Royal Gymnasium, one of the most remarkable and attractive places of amusement of its kind in Edinburgh, and few visitors leave the city without seeing it'. It was during the construction of the Gymnasium in 1865 that the loch was finally drained. 'At considerable expense', it was created by John Cox of Gorgie House 'for the purpose of affording healthful and exhilarating recreation in

The arch through which the north-bound trains emerged from Scotland Street Tunnel near the top of Broughton Road.

the open air' to large numbers of people at the same time. John Cox was the owner of Gorgie Mills and his mother was the sister of George Combe and his brother Andrew. Andrew held the appointment of physician to Queen Victoria while George had also achieved some fame as a moral philosopher and a phrenologist. The public opening of the Gymnasium, in April 1865, was attended by 'the provosts, magistrates and councillors of Edinburgh and Leith, accompanied by all the leading inhabitants of the city and county'. The cost of admission was 'very moderate', being 6d for adults and 3d for children under twelve.

The principal feature was a large round pond containing a Patent Rotary Boat, known as the *Great Sea Serpent*, which was seated for 600 rowers who were able to embark, or disembark, at four separate piers. In order to obtain water for the pond the North British Railway Company had allowed Cox to divert into it a burn the course of which had become enclosed within the Scotland

Street Tunnel. When rowing began to pall, one could try one's prowess on the more adventurous 'Self-Adjusting Trapeze' which enabled gymnasts, according to their advertisements, to swing by the hands, like seasoned acrobats, 'a distance of 130 feet from one trapeze to the other'. 'Holds about 100 persons and is kept in motion by those upon it' was their description of the Patent Compound Pendulum Swing, and, when they were about it, what youthful enthusiasts would be able to resist the temptation to be hoist on the Giant's Sea-Saw 'Chang' which, 100 feet long by 7 broad, could elevate 200 people to a height of 50 feet?

After such high-flying and apparently hazardous experiences, which also included a ride on the Patent Velocipede Paddle Merry-go-Round propelled by the feet of 600 'passengers', 'Horizontal and Rotary Ladders, Parallel Bars, Vaulting Poles, Sloping-Sliding Ropeways, Stilts, Quoits and Balls' offered exercise of a more tame if slightly less nerve-racking nature. The velocipede, it may be mentioned, was the forerunner of the bicycle. Invented around 1840 by a blacksmith from Dumfries called Macmillian, it consisted of two large wheels, the rear one being larger than the front, which were foot-operated by means of cranks and levers which thus propelled the rider and enabled him to control its speed.

Bands were also provided and special events were catered for, but all this activity had to take place, of necessity, in summer, and it proved difficult to protect the 'Velocipedes' and other contrivances throughout winter weather. Though well supported in its earlier years it became neglected and run-down by the late 1880s and the site was eventually taken over, in stages, by St Bernard's Football Club, known locally as the 'Saints'. They put up a stand on the east side of their pitch and employed a groundsman and trainer called Ross who took the 'pro-name' of Tom Brandon, presumably from nearby Brandon Street. He lived in 'Royal Gymnasium

Cottage, Royal Crescent', although the house was situated at the lower level of the old Haugh.

The army moved in after the outbreak of the First World War, however, leaving it, when they departed, in an unplayable condition. The 'Saints' did their best to put matters right, raising money by renting it to amateur clubs, but they could not afford full-time players and relied on their great popularity in Canonmills to draw large attendances, each supporter paying a shilling at the turnstile.

During the early part of the Second World War St Bernard's had to struggle to remain alive; they played their last match on 16 May 1942 and were not revived when the war came to an end in 1945. Juliet Rees, in *Once Upon a Haugh*, written to raise funds for the Scotland Yard Adventure Centre, concluded that, with the demise of the 'Saints', 'Perhaps the last remnants of the village community spirit in Canonmills had also been removed'.

The old dry basin of Canonmills Loch, when looking down into and across it from Royal Crescent, is still quite clearly discernible in spite of the western end having been claimed by the ubiquitous office builders in the last few years. At Gymnasium House in Fettes Row, a short continuation of the Row across Dundas Street before it curves into and becomes Royal Crescent, Macdonald's Dancing Academy was run by Mrs J.D. Macdonald before the Second World War. She and her husband succeeded Mr Macdonald's father as proprietors, when they lived in Perth Street, but the founder appears to have been James Symons who is listed in the Post Office Directory for 1900 as of 'Royal Gymnasium Hall'. By the 1940s it had become Macdonald's Ballroom under the name of Mrs Macdonald only, and it was closed down around 1960. The site of the St Bernard's Football Club lay for some time in a forlorn and neglected condition on the largely derelict old Haugh, although a house and a row of outbuildings were still in a reasonable state of preservation

The now demolished Alexander's Garage in Dundas Street. To its right can be seen the also demolished house built on the Canonmills Haugh and approached by a gate and a flight of steps. The pillar box is still there but has been moved to the back of the pavement. (Photograph courtesy The Michael Laird Partnership)

in 1980. Steps with a handrail led down from a low hedge in Dundas Street to the house, which latterly accommodated two families and was probably built at the west end of the Haugh before the turn of the century as Mr Symons is known to have lived in it when he owned the Ballroom, his aged father tending the terraced garden below the hedge. A short flight of steps can today be seen at approximately the same place on the north side of the Royal Bank of Scotland's new Computer Centre which was completed in 1981 on the northern corner of Fettes Row and Dundas Street, to make way for which the house, which was of no architectural significance, was taken down. The large, light-coloured office building, designed by The Michael Laird Partnership, rises in steps or stages, like a Babylonian ziggurat, from the original loch level and is entered from Fettes Row. 'Recycled wastage', says *Edinburgh: An Illustrated Architectural Guide* 1992, 'from the computers provides the heat'. It was followed, on the west side of Dundas Street, by BUPA and Sutherland Houses, which are next door neighbours with another office built for the Standard Life Assurance Company who have also built the only slightly later Tanfield House beside the Water of Leith of which an account is given later. In Dundas Street at the south-west corner of Eyre Place a building occupied by MacVitties, Guest & Co. Ltd was demolished and replaced in 1966 by a warehouse for Thomas Brown Bros, a wholesale motor accessories company. In 1982 the warehouse was 'wrapped up in brown anodised facing panels' (*The Buildings of Scotland: Edinburgh*) for the Trustee Savings Bank.

Another insurance company, The Life Association of Scotland, has built its new Head Office between the Trustee Savings Bank and the Royal Bank of Scotland on a site previously occupied (in an Art Deco building of 1931) by the car dealers Alexanders of Edinburgh Ltd and before that by John Player and Sons, the coach and motor hirers. This new building, with a row of frontal columns, is one of several which are floodlit at night.

These six office elevations face each other across Dundas Street, a principal traffic route through North Edinburgh, just beyond the north termination of the Northern New Town and their construction provided a splendid opportunity for the provision of imaginative late-twentieth century architectural excellence which was in empathy with its surroundings. All built in the 1980s, their styles have been given the blanket description of 'the modern look' but these haphazard structures, which make no attempt to blend with or complement each other, would have been anathema to the architects of the Georgian New Town and the words which come most readily to mind when judging their visual impact are 'unfortunate' and 'a missed opportunity'.

A Scottish artist receiving some recognition at the present day was brought up in Fettes Row. This was James
Pryde (1866 - 1941), the son of David Pryde, MA, LL.D,
headmaster of the Edinburgh Ladies' College (now the
Mary Erskine School) then at 70 and 72 Queen Street.
The family lived at No. 10 Fettes Row and they appear
to have stayed previously at No. 22 when James's father
was a lecturer on English literature in the School of Arts.
Subsequent to attending George Watson's College, James
left Edinburgh at an early age to study in Paris and then
to settle in London to which Dr Pryde and his family
had moved in the 1890s. After an unsuccessful attempt
to establish himself as an actor, he turned to painting,
his work being strongly influenced by, among that of
other places, the architecture of his native city. An exhibition of paintings and spectacular poster designs by
James Pryde was held in the Scottish National Gallery of
Modern Art during the 1992 Edinburgh Festival.

Henry Raeburn Dobson, the portrait painter and
brother of the artist Cowan Dobson, lived at No. 5 Fettes
Row for some years until his death around the 1980s.

An earlier artist to live for a short time in Fettes Row
was Leith-born Erskine Nicol, RSA (1825 - 1904). After
a few years in Dublin painting Irish subjects he returned
to Edinburgh, staying first at No. 13 and then at No.
15 Fettes Row from 1854 to 1856 in which latter year
No. 15 was a studio only. In 1861 he moved to London
and died at Feltham in Middlesex aged 78.

Edinburgh Corporation was determined that the building contractors were to be excluded from that part of
the Haugh which lay in front of Eyre Place when plans
for this area were being considered. The old Gymnasium
site was to become one of the many King George V Memorial Parks being created throughout the country and
an application was made to the National Playing Fields
Association for financial assistance. The estimated cost
was £10,000. 'Of this', writes Juliet Rees, '£1,350 was

Scotland Yard with, beyond, the King George V Memorial Park.

for the purchase of the ground, £6,000 for fencing, walls, memorial gates and furnishings, and £800 for a children's playground with swings, rocking horses and a merry-go-round'—a pale reflection, perhaps, of the circus which, with a Grand Top and side shows and other amusements, was held on the Haugh in the 1920s. On 11 May 1950 the official opening ceremony was performed by the President of the Scottish Branch of the National Playing Fields Association, the Duke of Buccleuch. The park included tennis courts, a putting green and a rose garden. 'Over the next three and a half decades', continues Juliet Rees, 'the story of the King George V Park is similar to that of the Gymnasium. Well used and appreciated at first, it was gradually allowed to become run down and overgrown'. Alongside it, to the east, attempts were being made to utilise the old station yard as a play area for children, but money was not available to do this satisfactorily.

The name of Scotland Yard had come into use for the children's play area and, when a committee was formed to develop this site in the 1980s, it became, officially, the Scotland Yard Adventure Centre—'a private limited company with charitable status established in 1986'. After clearing the old station and goods yard, trees were planted in December of that year to mark the 220th anniversary of the death of George Drummond, Lord Provost of the city at the time when the New Town of Edinburgh was being planned but who, having been born in 1687, did not live to see his dreams of a great development to the north of the Old Town come to fruition. The tennis courts and putting green have now gone from the Park. Laid out as a garden with paths and plants, it has become a western extension of the Adventure Centre which is itself affiliated to the Scottish Adventure Playgrounds Association for Handicapped Children, an organisation which had done much to help improve the park. It was visited by the Princess Royal on 14 June 1989. Four years later, on 19 October 1993, the Princess returned officially to open the improved and expanded Scotland Yard Adventure Centre which now has the distinction of being the first such centre in Edinburgh specifically planned to meet the needs of handicapped children and those with learning difficulties. This final phase of the scheme included the incorporation of the former rail yard, the sealing off of the southern entrance to the tunnel, the erection of a single-storey, steel span building for the purposes of both the education and the amusement of children and the enclosure of the whole area, which extends to three-quarters of an acre, within secure fencing. The cost of the building itself was £300,000 and towards this sum contributions were received from the BBC *Children in Need Appeal* (£200,000), the Scottish Office (£25,000) and corporate and individual donations. The building and its environs were designed by the Holmes Partnership of Leith.

The site of Canonmills Haugh in 1972.

The entrance to the park is at the foot of Logan Street on the south-east side of Eyre Place and it is here that the King George V Memorial Gates are situated. A unicorn is carved on the east pier and a crowned lion on the west pier, both holding shields. The carving is unfortunately already becoming badly weathered. On the inside of the gate an inscription reads:

National Playing Fields Association with the agreement of City of Edinburgh District Council is pleased to acknowledge that Wimpey Homes Holdings Ltd has generously 'ADOPTED' this recreation ground for the benefit of the community. 4.9.91.

The site of Canonmills Haugh in 1992.

Logan Street was built around the year 1909 on land owned by Thomas Anderson of Easter Road who probably called it after the Logans of Restalrig.

A large area of the former Haugh is now a car park for the Royal Bank of Scotland and part of the old loch with its perch and waterfowl, its fishermen and fowlers, has been replaced by serried rows of commuter cars.

Between Dundas Street and Logan Street the short Eyre Terrace runs southwards from Eyre Place and here a curious Edwardian property with two tall frontal chimney stacks can still be seen at Nos. 3-5. It is described in *The Buildings of Scotland: Edinburgh* as 'an improbable tenement of 1904, four rendered storeys, the surrounds stuck with bits of road-metal, a centre panel of a lion rampant between diamond panels with a thistle and a rose, all picked out with little coloured rocks.' In a footnote it is revealed that Sir Robert Lorimer 'supported the Dean of Guild petition, but can hardly have been the architect'. Behind the tenement, and entered through a

pend in the middle of it, is a workplace area which once
housed the Patriothall Laundry. Patriothall was the name
given to 'a symmetrical U-plan block of brick industrial
housing' built in 1861 on the south side of Hamilton
Place in Stockbridge, a well-planned and picturesque enclave, entered through a much larger pend, which is still
in use. It has three round-arched stair-towers, the central
one with a pyramidal roof, and 'cantilevered galleries for
access' to the upper flats. It takes its name from a house
called Patriot Hall which was still in existence here in
1827 but which was subsequently swept away.

It was here in Stockbridge that the laundry was
founded, possibly by David Peters who was the proprietor
in 1900. He may well have been responsible for the

Nos. 3-5 Eyre Terrace showing the Patriothall panels. The central
lion rampant is dated 1904.

building in Eyre Terrace as he moved there in 1904, the year when it was built, taking the old name of Patriothall with him. It then became the Patriothall Laundry and Bleachworks and Peters himself lived conveniently nearby at No. 12 Eyre Crescent. He must have employed only women, who would live, no doubt with their families, in the tenement flats, as the Post Office Directories state, by way of additional information, 'Laundresses and Clear Starchers'.

It must be supposed that the very prominent panels on the front of the building were put there, as emblems of patriotism, to emphasis the name and possibly even to advertise the laundry. In 1991 structural repairs were carried out, with scaffolding across the frontage, and, although the lion rampant with the date 1904 is still there, the two diamond panels, one of which contained a thistle and the other a rose, are now blank. For a short time, after the demolition of the garage premises prior to the building of the Royal Bank of Scotland offices, these panels were visible from Dundas Street.

CHAPTER 2

West Canonmills

A Canonmills landmark in the later years of the eighteenth century was Haig's Whisky Distillery located at the top of Glenogle Road (originally known, from its proximity to the Water of Leith, as Water Lane) and founded by James Haig, as their first distillery in Edinburgh, towards the end of the 1770s. Glenogle House, probably built by the Haigs, is now incorporated into the terraces of the Stockbridge Colonies built (between 1861 and 1911 on an area of land known formerly as The Whins), bought (at low cost and by instalments) and occupied by the artisans themselves who carved the implements of their various trades on the gables facing Glenogle Road. The Whins had been a favourite place for skirmishes, on the banks of the river, between the children of Canonmills and their arch-rivals in Stockbridge.

In 1783, a year of great scarcity of food in Edinburgh due, among other causes, to a bad harvest, this was the scene of meal-mob rioting after a report was circulated that 'great quantities of oats and potatoes' were being bought for the distillery. This aroused an angry crowd, bent on wrecking the Haig premises, to march down to Canonmills where the distillery employees were quickly issued with firearms and the Riot Act was read by the Sheriff. It was even decided to mobilise the servants in the country houses around Edinburgh, if need arose, to put down the disorder. A few days later the mob reappeared, this time to the ominous beat of drums, but by then the military had been called out and they were rapidly driven off.

At the height of this disturbance a coachman attempted to drive his carriage through the milling rioters but,

Heriot Hill House still retains much the same appearance as it had when this engraving was made for *Old and New Edinburgh* by James Grant.

convinced that members of the Haig family were inside, it was stopped by the mob who demanded to be told the identity of the occupants. The blinds had been drawn down over the windows but the door was rudely opened to reveal an unaccompanied lady in an understandable state of some anxiety. As she had no connection with the Haigs she was permitted to proceed and arrived without further incident at her destination of Heriot Hill House, the residence of her uncle. She subsequently became Mrs Hunter and the mother of the Sheriff of Dumbarton and Bute.

Passing to other owners, the distillery, before and after the Second World War, served as maltings for Wm. Younger & Co. at No. 5 Glenogle Road where the cooperage of William Lindsay & Son Ltd. was also sited. By the 1960s only the Lindsay cooperage was left. When the buildings were demolished in the early 1970s they had been in a derelict condition for some time before their acquisition by Barrett, the building contractors, who developed the area as flats, when the last remnants of the famous Haig Distillery were swept from the scene. Of this family was Douglas (later Earl) Haig, Commander-in-Chief of the British Army in France during the First World War.

Glenogle Road enters Canonmills from Stockbridge beside the Water of Leith opposite the junction of Brandon Street (a continuation of Dundas Street) and Brandon Terrace where the buildings turn the corner with an attractively curving elevation. The street was built in 1822 but the terrace, between the corner and Huntly Street, is late Victorian. These streets were also laid out on the James Eyre estate.

At No. 3 Brandon Street can be read the carved inscription: 'Sir D'Arcy Thompson scholar, naturalist, was born here, 1860'. A classical scholar and a zoologist, Sir D'Arcy Wentworth Thompson (1860 - 1948) was educated at Edinburgh Academy just a short distance to the west in Henderson Row, Edinburgh University and Trinity College, Cambridge. When aged 24, he was appointed Professor of Biology at the then new University of Dundee and, in 1917, was given the senior Chair of Natural History at the United College of St Andrews and Dundee. The recipient of many honours, he wrote a number of works on biology and was President of the Royal Society of Edinburgh from 1934 - 39.

Across the road at No. 20 are the former printing works, built about 1883, of R. & R. Clark which were redeveloped in the late 1970s. Only the Jacobean facade, ornamented with somewhat shallow strapwork carving and spiky upper-floor window pediments, has been retained as part of a courtyard layout on ground which stands above Glenogle Road on the north and faces Perth Street on the west. This building is now occupied by the

Post Office, the Edinburgh-based British Philatelic Bureau
and Historic Scotland which administers all listed monuments in the care of the Secretary of State for Scotland
and will move to the former Longmore Hospital in Salisbury Place in the near future. The new complex was
opened in March 1979. It is interesting to note that there
was an artificial curling pond at the north end of Perth
Street, which was floodlit at night at the turn of the century. It is shown on maps of that period but the site is
now obliterated by office buildings.

Directly opposite Eyre Place across Dundas Street is
Henderson Row, called after Alexander Henderson, Lord
Provost of Edinburgh from 1823 - 25 and the founder
of the National Bank of Scotland and the Union Assur-
ance Company. A seed merchant who lived in Warriston
House, he came into conflict with the Princes Street pro-
prietors over his nursery in part of Princes Street
Gardens. At the presentation ceremony when the freedom
of the city was granted to Lord Brougham Alexander
Henderson was in the chair.

The Edinburgh Academy was founded in Henderson
Row in the 1820s in the austere neo-Greek building by
William Burn which stands, within an ample forecourt,
on the north side, in spite of the controversy by which
its origins were surrounded. When the construction of a
new school was under consideration by the city fathers,
a site at Canonmills was suggested for a 'seminary separate from and altogether independent of the High School.'
But this proposal was set aside and it was decided that
what was needed was a new High School. Burn was engaged to prepare drawings and the site of the present
Academy was accepted as its location. Shortly afterwards,
however, the Town Council 'changed its position,' being
now of the opinion, as A.J. Youngson writes in *The
Making of Classical Edinburgh*, 'that to site a new school
near Canonmills would be "most exceedingly inconvenient
for the inhabitants at large," however convenient it might

be for pupils in the New Town, and that in any case a second school would so reduce numbers at the old school that "its progress to ruin will be incalculably accelerated." There should, therefore, be only one school, in a central position.' So a site for the new High School was chosen on Calton Hill where this turn of events gave another architect, Thomas Hamilton, the opportunity to design a masterpiece; and that, they thought, was the end of the matter.

But the original subscribers, Sir Walter Scott and Lord Cockburn among them, were determined that their plans should go ahead and the Edinburgh Academy was built, in defiance of the Town Council, and opened in October 1824. Its troubles, however, were not over. The building contractor, having run out of money and discharged his workmen, died, and the school was not completed till the Spring of 1829, the final cost being £24,200 'not an excessive sum,' says Youngson, 'for a building which has been described as "the noblest monument of the Scottish Greek Revival" '.

Cumberland Hill, the historian of Stockbridge, recalls the short and brilliant life of one of the Academy's most outstanding pupils. George Rankin Luke was born in Brunswick Street (now St Stephen Street) in March 1836, the son of James Luke, a master baker. George took all the prizes at Hamilton Place Academy and in 1845 was entered at Circus Place School where the rector said of him that 'he was one of a thousand.' Transferring to the Edinburgh Academy, where he remained during the years 1847 - 53, the prize lists there became 'studded with Luke's name' and, after becoming Dux of the school in the latter year, he went on first to Glasgow University and then to Balliol College, Oxford, where his academic successes were continued. But they were tragically cut short when, on 3rd March 1862, at the age of twenty-six, he was drowned as a consequence of the overturning of a boat on the River Isis. Deeply mourned in both

The Edinburgh Academy (from *Old and New Edinburgh* by James Grant)

England and Scotland, the far-reaching influences he would have exerted in whatever career he had intended to take up were never to be known.

It was widely believed at the time, or at least so it was said, that the Town Council, in revenge for this flouting of their civic authority, built the burgh church of St Stephen's (in 1827 by W.H. Playfair) with its tall clock tower at the foot of St Vincent Street some 260 yards, says Grant, south of the low, single-storey Academy with the deliberate intention of blocking the excellent view of it which would otherwise have been obtained down Frederick Street and Howe Street.

The Edinburgh Deaf and Dumb Institution, which had been founded by subscription in 1819, was built on a site immediately to the west of the Academy in an area formerly known as Canonmills Park in the same year,

1823, that work commenced on this widely known boys' school. Designed by J. Gillespie Graham, the Institution stands, three storeys high, behind an extensive garden and was enlarged by the addition of two-storey wings in 1893. The foundation stone was laid, as Grant records, in May 1823 by one of the senior pupils 'in presence of his voiceless companions.' Children whose parents resided in Edinburgh or Leith were eligible to become day pupils, and were instructed in the same branches of learning as their less disabled contemporaries, on payment of such fees as were determined by the directors.

Prior to the Second World War it had become the Royal Deaf and Dumb Institution and in 1939, its work having been taken over by the later but much larger Donaldson's School for the Deaf, that name had also been given to the Institution which became the Junior Department of Donaldson's School under the Institution's current Headmaster, Mr G.A. Sutcliffe, and subsequently their Nursery and Infant Department. The final change came in 1977 when the building was sold to the Edinburgh Academy to provide them with additional accommodation and all educational facilities for the deaf were located within the Donaldson building, originally Donaldson's Hospital. This princely edifice, for which Queen Victoria once expressed her admiration, stands in its own spacious grounds at West Coates on the western side of Haymarket. Designed by Playfair in an amalgam of English Elizabethan and Jacobean styles between 1841 and '51, Donaldson's Hospital was funded from the bequest of James Donaldson, a printer who lived in Broughton Hall and who left a sum of approximately £210,000 on his death in 1830 for the purpose of establishing an orphan hospital which later specialised in the teaching of deaf children.

It having been discovered that dumbness was the result of an inability to hear rather than an inability to speak, a great deal of successful work has gone into the training

of deaf children to use their voices and the word 'Dumb'
was therefore dropped from the titles of such institutions.

In 1968 the Henderson Row building featured as the
Marcia Blaine School for Girls during the filming of *The
Prime of Miss Jean Brodie*, when the name of Muriel
Spark's fictitious school appeared over the entrance in an
ironwork arch between the gate piers.

On the south side of Henderson Row, at No. 57, the
power station and depot of the Edinburgh Northern
Tramways Company was built in 1886 to serve the north
side of the city. The architect was W. Hamilton Beattie
(1840 - 98), the noted designer of hotels including the
North British (now Balmoral) at the east end of Princes
Street where, on the opposite side, he was Charles Jenner's
architect for the rebuilding of his famous Renaissance-style
department store in 1893. To the west, adjoining the
power station, a public Wash House, the forerunner of
the present-day launderette, was built in 1904. The depot
was the first of four such buildings eventually provided
from which all the city's underground cables were driven
by the steam engines housed within them, the other three
being at Tollcross, Shrubhill and Portobello. Hanover and
Frederick Streets and their northward continuations were
too steep for the horse-drawn trams, which required the
assistance of trace-horses (a boy always accompanied a
trace-horse so that he could ride it back to its base after
the hill had been negotiated) on the southern journey, and
on 28 January 1888 a cable route was opened from Hanover Street to Goldenacre via Canonmills and Inverleith.
The Frederick Street to Stockbridge and Comely Bank
route followed in 1890. Using a total of twenty-five cable
cars, the northern services proved so successful initially that
cable traction was adopted for the whole of Edinburgh.

As explained in *A History of Edinburgh Transport:*

The complex layout of the Edinburgh tramway system made operation by cable peculiarly difficult. In the agreement with the operating firm, it was stipulated that the junctions had to be worked without resort to gravity operation. This meant that geared down auxiliary cables had to be laid at sharp corners. Each car was fitted at either end with a double-sided gripper suspended through the slot between the rails. The jaws were regulated by the driver with a control wheel, to engage or release the underground steel cable as required. In order to proceed round acute curves at a reduced speed, the driver released the main cable and picked up the auxiliary cable geared down on pulleys to a slower speed. After releasing the auxiliary cable the main cable was again picked up by the gripper.

The former Edinburgh Northern Tramways Company cable car Depot in Henderson Row in 1982.

Breakdowns, however, on the northern and other routes began to happen with increasing frequency, incurring barbed comments from the long-suffering passengers, and the Henderson Row depot was finally closed down in 1922 when buses were used until electric trams, which had first been introduced in the city in 1910, were substituted. The current was supplied by overhead wires which were engaged by means of a trolley on the car roof which was detached and reattached manually by the driver when it was required to reverse the direction in which it was to travel.

The old Edinburgh Northern Tramways Company had been promoted in 1884 by a group of local landowners anxious to get a more satisfactory transport system for the North Side. A short section of both cable tracks and the later tram lines was preserved in the roadway at the western end of Waterloo Place where they can still be seen.

The Henderson Row Depot, after several changes of use from housing Corporation buses to a lock-up garage to an electricity transformer sub-station to a public washhouse, became a police garage and vehicle pound which it remained until the site was bought in 1986 by The Scottish Life Assurance Company, whose Head Office, of which the new Silvermills Building is an extension, is in St Andrew Square. It was then demolished although the facade, with the words 'Edinburgh Corporation Tramways' carved below the roofline, has been retained. The two-storeyed cottages which stood beside the depot were built for the Cable Tramways engineers and these living quarters were later used by the chauffeur of the Lord Provost's car.

The splendid French Empire-style, four-storey building, part of a £13 million pound development by the company on this site, is much larger than the old Power Station and occupies an extended area opposite Perth Street. With black-painted cast iron colonnade and balconies, it integrates well into its Georgian and Victorian surroundings and its origins are recalled by an inscribed panel on the wall of the former depot which reads:

> This building constructed in 1991 by The Scottish Life Assurance Company retains the facade of the 1888 depot and powerhouse of The Edinburgh Northern Tramways Company. Cable tramcars from this depot ran from Princes Street to Goldenacre and Stockbridge until 1920.

Round the corner in Henderson Place two iron wheels from this period have been exposed at the side of the building with the accompanying inscription:

> This pulley unit was part of the equipment installed by the Edinburgh Northern Tramways Company to carry the cables for cable tramcars operated from the Depot on this site from 1888 to 1920.

Housing built out on the east side of the Silvermills Building preserves a pulley unit used in the former cable car power station and depot.

Designed by The Kennedy Partnership, among the difficulties to be overcome before building could commence was the relocation of a New Town electricity sub-station without any disruption of the supply of electricity! The intention to plant trees along the front of the building had to be abandoned on account of the amount of underground electrical equipment here, and their place has been taken by a large, black iron planter which has proved to be a most acceptable substitute. Because of the made-up nature of the ground the building itself had to be erected on piles to obtain a solid base for the foundations. It was officially opened by HRH the Princess Royal on 9 November 1992.

Other buildings, including the company's printing and supplies department and Silvermills Court, which is rented as a number of separate units, have been built behind in a style complementary to the main building.

On the other side of Henderson Row Perth Street, erected shortly after 1825, runs to the north and terminates above Glenogle Road.

A newspaper advertisement for the sale of several properties in Henderson Row in 1828, not long after they were built, describes the houses as elegant and superior and the street itself as combining the advantages of both town and country. The Edinburgh Academy and the 'Botanical Gardens' are included in a list of amenities in the neighbourhood, and, 'the street being open and healthful, with a southern exposure, like Princes Street, it is as desirable a residence as any in Edinburgh.' The ground on which Henderson Row was built had been feued from James Eyre. If it was less fashionable to live just outside the New Town it was also less expensive, as the proprietors of the Eyre development were subject to a lower assessment than their New Town neighbours. This fact was made much of in such advertisements.

The area bounded by Dundas Street, Henderson Row, Clarence and St Stephen Streets, and Fettes Row encom-

A rear view of the large and elegant Silvermills Building of The Scottish Life Assurance Company, built in 1991. The pulley unit can be seen on the right of the building in Henderson Place. (Photograph courtesy The Scottish Life Assurance Company)

passes what remains of the tiny village of Silvermills which clustered, wrote James Grant, 'by the ancient mill-lade and which of old lay within the Barony of Broughton.' West Silvermills Lane represents part of Gabriel's Road and in it, opposite Silvermills House, is a derelict building, painted red, which has the date 1714 on a wall projection and scrolled skewputts which can still be made out on the south-facing gable. It may yet be rescued as it has permission for office development. At the foot of East Silvermills Lane on the eastern side is an old iron gas bracket which has been converted (and is still in use) into one of the earliest electric street lamps in Edinburgh. And further east at the junction with Henderson Place Lane can be seen the lower storeys of an eighteenth century house which were used as the base for part of the Victorian housing in Henderson Row, where,

Behind the modern red paint is a house, dated 1714, in West Silvermills Lane which may possibly be rescued from dereliction and converted to office use.

at No. 69, two small gate-piers mark what was probably the original back of the house, its name having apparently slipped into oblivion.

The derivations of these street names are of interest. Henderson Row has already been mentioned and Pitt Street, the former name of lower Dundas Street, recalls William Pitt (1759 - 1806), usually known as 'the Younger' to distinguish him from his father who became the first Earl of Chatham. The younger Pitt took on his prime ministerial duties at the age of 25 in 1784. Dundas Street was called after Henry Dundas, Viscount Melville (1742 - 1811), Member of Parliament for Midlothian and Home Secretary in 1791. He was the most important and influential politician in Scotland in the years around 1800 and a monument was erected to his memory, on a column 150 feet high, in St Andrew Square Gardens. King William IV (1765 - 1837) who, prior to his accession, was the Duke of Clarence, gave his name to Clarence

Early street lighting by electricity from a converted gas bracket in East Silvermills Lane.

Street, and St Stephen's Church provided an alternative for St Stephen Street which was formerly Brunswick Street. (The main mill-lade, running into Silvermills, passed through the gap site at Nos 21 - 25 Clarence Street and a recent proposal for residential infilling of the gap has been withdrawn.)

Among the title deeds of St Stephen's Church is a contract of excambion, or exchange of land, dated 1823, between Edinburgh Corporation and John Lauder, tanner in Silvermills, of whom more will be said shortly, and on this land, described later by Ian G. Lindsay as 'a difficult site,' rose Playfair's unusual and imaginative church—a square set diagonally to St Vincent Street with an octagonal interior. A clock, which it was, after much debate, decided to illuminate with gas (the pendulum, as The Rev. A. Ian Dunlop describes it in *The Kirks of Edinburgh*, being 'probably the longest in the country'), was placed in its tall and pinnacled tower, while the entrance, at the top of a long flight of steps, led into the gallery beneath which a false floor was some years ago inserted when the gallery became the church and the former church became the church halls. St Stephen's was dedicated, in the presence of the Lord Provost and Magistrates, on 21st December 1828. The intended street layout here was that St Vincent Street should, in the words of Lord Sands in his history of the church, 'sweep round into Fettes Row on the east, just as it sweeps round into St Stephen Street on the west.' That it does not is, he observes, 'a most unfortunate divergence from the original plan.' It may well have been made impossible by the positioning of the church.

The clock tower of the former St Stephen's Parish Church at the foot of St Vincent Street. It contains one of the longest pendulums in the country.

Did R.L.S. recall his family's connection with St Stephen's when he wrote *Catriona*? In the story, the sequel to *Kidnapped*, the adventures of the principal characters are continued and David Balfour and Alan Breck, who had parted in the first volume on Corstorphine Hill, met again in the second 'Besouth of the mill-lade in a scrog of wood.' It was the 'scrog of wood' that became the site on which St Stephen's Church was built.

The Deaf and Dumb Institution in Henderson Row was within the parish of St Stephen's and, before they obtained their own place of worship in Albany Street (which is still there), 'the deaf mutes,' as Lord Sands called them, 'worshipped in St Stephen's School.' Special Communion Services were held for them 'between the forenoon and afternoon tables,' at which the sacraments were dispensed with the assistance of an interpreter.

Sir William Fettes (1750 - 1836), a grocer at the head of Bailie Fyfe's Close in the High Street, was the name-father of Fettes Row. He was Lord Provost in 1800 and owned the estate of Comely Bank on which was built that other famous boys' school on the north side of Edinburgh, Fettes College, in the 1860s. The Battles of Cape St Vincent were fought by Admiral Rodney (hence Rodney Street) in 1780 and by Admiral Howe (hence Howe Street) in 1784 and gave their name to St Vincent Street.

The small industrial enclave of Silvermills was chiefly occupied by tanners whose skills were in such demand that when the New Town was expanding in its direction in the 1820s the hamlet, which would otherwise have been sacrificed to the street and terrace builders, was saved from obliteration. Robert Chambers, in *Traditions of Edinburgh*, describes the ancient Gabriel's Road, already mentioned, which diagonally crossed the New Town on its way to Stockbridge, and what little is left of it now includes the steps which lead down from Saxe-Coburg Place to Glenogle Road, the termination of the old way which provided access to the city for the tanners and other villagers who included weavers, tailors and blacksmiths. There were even orchards in the area as well. Much later in date than Stockbridge, most of the land was owned by Heriot's Hospital by 1760.

Silvermills achieved some fame in the early seventeenth century when, in 1607, deposits of silver were discovered at Hilderstone, in West Lothian, on property in the Bathgate Hills owned by the Earl of Haddington who sank a shaft for the mining of the ore. It received considerable publicity and news of the existence of the mine soon reached the ears of King James VI and I in London. James, being chronically short of money, paid the Earl five thousand pounds and took possession of the workings. By this time, however, the mine was becoming less productive and, in spite of importing Cornish tin miners and even employees of the silver mines of Saxony, 'the King,' says Chambers, 'withdrew from the enterprise a great loser.' But before he did so he had set up a mill on the Water of Leith 'for the melting and fining of the ore' which, as a consequence, acquired the name of Silvermills.

East and West Silvermills Lanes now lead down to the all but vanished hamlet, the latter terminating at the three-storey, rubble-built Silvermills House dating from around 1760, the only substantial building to have survived. It was built by Nicol Somerville, a merchant, who moved to Silvermills because he saw it as the home of a prosperous and industrious community. The next owner was the skinner and tanner John Lauder who built, quotes A.J. Youngson, 'a new manufactory with a steam engine, on a large scale for manufacturing and preparing Shoe Leather, Sheepskin, Buff Leather and glue' which tended to be 'offensive, noxious and disagreeable to the neighbourhood,' although objections by feuars in Great King Street in 1812 to its erection do not appear to have been successful as nothing more was heard of them. It was in Silvermills House that his sons, Robert and James, who were both to achieve fame as prominent nineteenth

Scottish artists Robert Scott Lauder and his brother were born in the rubble-built Silvermills House which dates from c.1760.

century Scottish artists, were born and spent their childhoods.

Robert Scott Lauder, RSA (1803 - 69) and his brother James Eckford Lauder, RSA (1813 - 69) were the forerunners of a group which has been called the first genuine school of Scottish painting. Their master was Scott Lauder himself. Having trained at the Trustees' Academy in Edinburgh and also in London, he went to Italy in 1833 where he stayed for five years, returning to London in 1838 and to Edinburgh in 1852. During the 1850s he was Director of the Scottish Academy and many of his pupils, William MacTaggart and W.Q. Orchardson among them, became distinguished portraitists and landscape painters later in the century. He married a daughter of the famous landscape painter The Rev. John Thomson, Minister of Duddingston Kirk.

One of Robert's best-known portraits is of a younger brother, Henry, who died in 1827 at the age of twenty and it was probably painted in the year of his death. It shows a young man fashionably dressed in the style of the early nineteenth century with a somewhat serious, even sad, expression beneath a very large top hat. This portrait is frequently included in historical exhibitions of the work of Scottish painters.

On Robert Scott Lauder's death on 21st April 1869 his students subscribed towards a memorial to be placed above his tomb in Warriston Cemetery. A portrait head in high relief was executed by John Hutchison, who had studied sculpture under Lauder, but it proved necessary for a replica to be carved as the marble of the original was found to be flawed. The inscription reads, 'in grateful remembrance of his unfailing sympathy as a friend and able guidance as a master.' The work of his brother, James Eckford Lauder, is less well known although it also is included in exhibitions from time to time.

Their old house in Silvermills, now occupied by Strathearn Advertising Ltd, by whom it was restored, was approached along an avenue of 'venerable elms' and 'there was green sward in front' of it. Within there were panelled rooms and carved mantels. Much of the land had come into the possession of Somerville and Lauder by 1817 and it has been claimed that it was the success of the Lauder tannery which prevented the little village from being swallowed up by the New Town and which kept these light industries alive for much longer than would otherwise have been the case.

CHAPTER 3

Easter and Upper Canonmills

The east end of Brandon Terrace curves round to the south in the short but interesting Huntly Street. It was built in 1825 as part of Robert Brown's development of the Eyre estate and originally extended westwards to meet the northern end of Brandon Street (from the Dukes of Hamilton whose secondary title was Duke of Brandon). The large section opposite the Water of Leith was later renamed Brandon Terrace, reducing Huntly Street to its present truncated size. The tall, round-headed windows and fanlights here are gracefully ornamented by a decorative arrangement of curving astragals and create a striking contrast with the mid-nineteenth century baronialism on the other side of the street. Recent stone cleaning, and the insertion of one or two reproduction windows to preserve the symmetry, have greatly enhanced the appearance of these Huntly Street tenement facades.

The Victorian painter Joseph Bartholomew Kidd (1808 - 89) entered briefly into the annals of Canonmills when he resided at No. 6 Huntly Street from 1829 - 31, moving there from 16 East Drummond Street, where he had spent a year, and going on to No. 14 Henderson Row where he stayed during the years 1832 - 34. He was one of the original Associates of the Royal Scottish Academy in 1826 and was appointed an Academician three years later. On removing to London in 1836 he resigned from the R.S.A. with effect from 1838. Well known for his Highland landscapes and portraits, Kidd had been a pupil of The Rev. John Thomson of Duddingston and was latterly a drawing master at Greenwich where he lived until his death at the age of 81, having very shortly beforehand painted a portrait of Queen Victoria for the

The distinctive curved wall and ornamental astragals at Huntly Street, built in 1825.

Royal Hospital Schools in Greenwich. The flats at No. 6 Huntly Street face the entrance to Warriston Road beside the Water of Leith. (The house numbers in Henderson Row are known to have been altered many years ago and the number given here may therefore have been changed.)

Huntly Street got its name from the 4th Marquess of Huntly who married Lady Elizabeth Howard, daughter of the Duke of Norfolk, in 1676. Howard Place, earlier in date and just beyond Canonmills Bridge, was called after the Marquess's wife. Huntly Street 'turns a flat front to the foot of Canon Street' (*The Buildings of Scotland: Edinburgh*) from which it is separated by Canon Lane, a quiet backwater behind Brandon Terrace with rear gardens and their walls and trees and some mews properties. With an entrance only at the Huntly Street end, it curves towards, but does not connect with, Eyre Place. The tenements of Canon Street run up from the Esso Service

Station to the old Canon Mill, already referred to, at the top.

The conjunction of the Canonmills crossroads has been reached at Brandon Terrace and Huntly Street. Inverleith and the road to Trinity lie across the bridge to the north and Warriston Road starts eastwards from the south side of the bridge. The road to the south, above the hill rising from the river valley and bounded by the old wall of Heriot Hill House, is Rodney Street, (originally the Canonmills Road) taking its name from Admiral George Brydges Rodney, 1st Baron Rodney (1719 - 92) who saw distinguished service during the Napoleonic Wars and was made an honorary burgess of Edinburgh in 1781. A name which can still be seen in Rodney Street on the east side near the top of Broughton Road is The Stag's Head. In 1906 a newspaper article made reference to this tavern which was by then located here, the old premises having been swept away. The original Stag's Head had been the starting place for the coach to the north and a much frequented resort of the burghers of their day in 'the then quaint old village by the Water of Leith.'

On the west side of Rodney Street in recent times stood the Ritz Picture House, built by Scottish Cinema and Variety Theatres (later to become the nucleus of the ABC chain) and opened in September 1929 with *The Singing Fool*. As the Scotland Street Railway Tunnel runs directly underneath, it was necessary to incorporate steel girders in its construction to prevent the weight of the building from resting on top of the tunnel above which, in addition, there is a very shallow layer of soil. These factors have so far prevented any replacement, such as flats, from being introduced on the site which, as a result, has the unattractive appearance of a piece of waste ground.

The Ritz 'was designed for both silent and Talkie films. In the event, Talkies reached Edinburgh during its construction so the new Rodney Street house opened only

A cat enjoys the sunshine, and the peace, in the quiet backwater of Canon Lane.

for sound.' (*The Last Picture Shows—Edinburgh* by the late Brendon Thomas). It belonged latterly to EMI who decided to close it in order to concentrate on their other cinemas at the ABC Centre in Lothian Road. Only the stalls were in use during the last few years before its demise in November 1981 and 'applications for a bingo licence had been consistently refused.' The building was demolished in 1983.

To the south of the undeveloped cinema site are the Halls of St Mary's (now Broughton St Mary's) Parish Church in Bellevue Crescent. Built as St Mary's Parish School in 1830 by architect George Smith who was also a member of the congregation and did not charge for drawing up the plans, this was originally a smaller, single-storey building. A problem, however, was waiting to arise. About ten years later it was discovered that the proposed line of The Edinburgh, Leith and Newhaven Railway Company's Scotland Street Tunnel would run

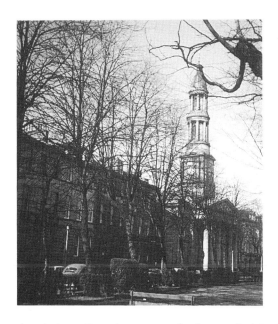

A Georgian church in a Georgian street—the former St Mary's Parish Church in Bellevue Crescent.

under the north-west corner of the school, causing concern for the safety of the children. A report by two civil engineers, one of them being David Stevenson, the son of Robert and uncle of R.L.S., was then prepared for the church but, as it was not reassuring, it was suggested to the railway company that they purchase the school when, with the proceeds of the sale, a new parochial school could be built elsewhere. But the tunnel went ahead without any change of ownership of the schoolhouse and no harm to building or children seems to have resulted. A toll bar once stood outside this building to mark the division between the New Town and the country beyond.

In 1872 School Boards, laying down minimum ages between which education was compulsory, took over the work so long and so faithfully conducted by the churches and in 1877, after five years under the aegis of the

Edinburgh School Board, St Mary's former Parish School was closed and the pupils transferred to the newly opened Stockbridge School.

George Smith's building being, by the 1880s, inadequate for the church's purposes, a second storey to the front only (the original hall has no building above it) was added in 1885 by Sydney Mitchell, one of the two architects employed by Patrick Geddes in his restoration projects in the Royal Mile. Having now a large gable, with outsize crowsteps above the second floor, facing Rodney Street, and a stair contained within a projection on the northern side, it had taken on its present appearance and today consists of two halls, one at each level.

In 1898, however, consideration was again given to its possible sale. As Messrs Neill & Co. Ltd (the printing works which had been owned by Dr Patrick Neill of Canonmills House) were constructing their new premises on adjoining ground at that time, enquiry was made as to whether they would be willing to buy it. Neill & Co. agreed and offered the church £1300 in settlement of the

Originally St Mary's Parochial School, this crow-stepped building with an interesting history later became the Parish Church halls.

bargain. But again difficulties intervened as it was by now all too clear that the Kirk Session had no power to dispose of their old schoolhouse, possession being vested in the subscribers, who had financed its erection, and their nominees. So it continued to be used as halls by the church until the union of St Mary's with Broughton McDonald Church in 1992 and it was sold, in June 1993, to the Central Branch of The Royal British Legion.

Canonmills Primary School, firstly under the management of the Edinburgh School Board, then of the Corporation Education Department and now of Lothian Regional Council's Department of Education, was built further up. A plain building designed by Robert Wilson, which was opened on 6 September 1880, it has the Edinburgh School Board figure of Education carved in a roundel on the central gable, but the bellcote with which it was originally provided has disappeared.

The school badge, in blue, purple, gold and white with a water wheel at the top and C S underneath, was approved by the Education Committee of the Town Council in October 1953. Just three years later, however, arrangements were made for the reorganisation of primary schools in north central Edinburgh with effect from 4 March 1957. The Canonmills pupils were then transferred to Broughton, Stockbridge and London Street Primary Schools and primary education at Canonmills School was discontinued. To mark its closure in 1957, after seventy-seven years as a primary school, a service for staff, pupils and parents was held in St Mary's Parish Church and was conducted by The Rev. Denis Lant of Dublin Street Baptist Church in the absence, due to illness, of The Rev. A.T. Laurence who was both minister of St Mary's and Chaplain of Canonmills School. The Headmaster, Mr Donald W.S. Mackenzie, then took up a similar position at Stockbridge School.

The name of the Canonmills building was then changed to Clarebank when the school for handicapped children of that name in Leith was transferred here temporarily while refurbishment of their own premises was taking place. Of Clarebank School John Russell writes, '. . . in 1919, when the Leith School Board handed over its schools to the newly constituted Education Authority, these schools numbered no fewer than eighteen, exclusive of three special schools,' one of which was 'at Clarebank for pupils whose health required special attention.' Reverting in 1978 to its own name of Canonmills School, it now provides educational facilities for children with special needs.

There is nothing new about the education of the young in Canonmills. At least as early as 1637 a certain Master Knox in Canonmylnis taught children 'to reid, wryte, an lay comptis.' In 1938 a large new school was planned for the area but, perhaps on account of the war, it never materialised.

On the east side of Rodney Street Heriot Hill Terrace was closed off at the eastern end by the Imperial Laundry until after the Second World War, and on the other, western, side, a flight of ten steps leads down to a long, narrow and unnamed passageway between the buildings, that on the left being on the site of Neill's printing works, then known as their Bellevue Factory, which was burned down in 1916, all that escaped being the suite of offices, a small two-storeyed building fronting Rodney Street. After the fire the business, under the name of Neill & Co. Ltd, was moved to No. 212 Causewayside where it remained until, the oldest printing house in Scotland (having commenced, as already noted, as early as 1749), its doors were closed in July 1973.

Although not bankrupt, heavy capital investment would have been required to enable them to change from the old letterpress printing to more modern methods, and the falling profitability of the industry and the growing competition from London were currents running strongly against their continuing survival. Neill's premises were sold to Ross Motors, a neighbouring company in Causewayside, and have recently been converted into flats.

The Bellevue Factory, in red sandstone, had the words 'Established 1749 Erected 1899' above the lintel, while a roundel displaying a carved head of Dr Patrick Neill within a wreath and surmounted by a ball finial was contained within a broken pediment. It is possible that part of a wall and some of the stone of the printing works were used in the construction of the Ritz Picture House. The story of Neill's firm is told in *The House of Neill*, edited by Moray McLaren and published to commemorate its 200th anniversary in 1949.

The area behind Rodney Street (to the rear of the former St Mary's Parish School and the vacant 'Ritz' site) and the site of the demolished Canonmills Cottage consists today of a car park, at the foot of which is situated the Waverley Biscuit Factory, and waste ground.

The narrow, unnamed passageway, probably a section of an old right of way skirting the loch at this point, emerges at the east end of Eyre Place. On Johnston's Plan of Edinburgh and Leith of 1851 a Toll Bar is shown on the south-east corner of Dundas Street and Eyre Place opposite Henderson Row.

The former church of the German congregation in Edinburgh stands at the corner of Rodney Street and Cornwallis Place. Now the Bellevue Chapel, it was designed by the Leith architect James B. Wemyss for Herr Johann Blumenreich and was opened in 1881. The foundation stone was laid by Lord Provost Sir Thomas Boyd in October 1879 in presence, says Grant, 'of a vast concourse of people.' The spire of this little Gothic-style church is visible across the lower end of Canonmills Haugh. In 1916, during the First World War, the fabric of this church was damaged in the course of a Zeppelin raid on the city. Throughout that period, however, when many Germans resident in Britain were interned, the members were unable to hold services and their building

passed to a small group of Brethren. The German congregation was not revived until after 1945 when they
were given temporary accommodation in Holy Trinity
Church at the Dean Bridge until they obtained their own
premises in Chalmers Crescent where the new German
Lutheran Church, designed by Alfred Schildt of Frankfurt,
was built in 1967 with an adjoining minister's house.
There has been a German-speaking congregation in Edinburgh since the mid-nineteenth century and they
worshipped in Queen Street Hall (at the rear of No. 5
Queen Street and now part of the premises of the BBC)
prior to the building of the church in Rodney Street with
a seating capacity of 350.

The spire which dominates eastern Canonmills, in the
same way as the west is dominated by the square tower
of St Stephen's, is the graceful, rounded steeple, on which
a four-dial clock was installed in 1826, of St Mary's Parish Church, built two years previously, in Bellevue
Crescent. Designed by Thomas Brown it was erected, like
St Stephen's, for the Town Council as a Burgh Church.
(The Act of Parliament authorising the second Royalty
extension required a third Burgh Church when the pop-
ulation of the new extension reached five thousand. St
Mary's had been preceded by St George's and St
Andrew's and was followed by St Stephen's, the fourth,
and, finally, by Greenside, the fifth. All Burgh Churches
were provided by the Town Council.) From behind an
impressive hexastyle Corinthian portico St Mary's faces
East Claremont Street and, with the garden layout in
front of the Crescent, is the focal point of a balanced
and eye-catching composition. It is fortunate in retaining
its original pulpit, now slightly lowered, and, with some
pews and the precentor's box the only missing features,
it presents an interior remarkably, although not entirely,
unmodified since it was first built.

The name of Robert Stevenson (1772 - 1850), the
lighthouse engineer and grandfather of Robert Louis Ste-

venson, who lived at No. 1 Baxter's Place at the top of Leith Walk, is recorded in the seat rent rolls although his pew was unfortunately among those removed during minor alterations to the interior. The family subsequently transferred first to Greenside Parish Church and then to St Stephen's where Robert Louis's father was Session Clark and his mother one of the most active workers in the congregation. It was here that his early boyish stories were first presented to an audience when Mrs Stevenson proudly read them to the Mothers' Meetings at St Stephen's.

In August 1992 the congregation of St Mary's united with that of the nearby Broughton McDonald (formerly Broughton Place) to form Broughton St Mary's Parish Church, and later the same year the congregation of St Stephen's united with that of St Bernard's to form Stockbridge Church, the historic St Stephen's building now being used for community purposes and its Willis organ for recitals.

Beside the gardens on the north side of the open space in front of St Mary's Church is a public seat set on a low platform, a feature which is absent from the seat on the opposite side. This platform originally supported a water trough, narrow and bath-like in shape, for the tradesmen's horses which could still be seen here in the 1940s or '50s. They were once a familiar sight on the streets of Edinburgh and were no doubt appreciated, especially in hot weather, by the hard-working cart horses delivering coal and other merchandise throughout the city.

Cornwallis Place, a short street at the eastern end of the Haugh, commemorates the 1st Marquess of Cornwallis (1738 - 1805). A soldier of distinction and a Member of Parliament, he is mainly remembered for his capitulation to American troops in 1781, thus securing independence for America and the end of its colonial status.

On the east side of the hill leading down to Canonmills Bridge, at the junction with Broughton Road, stands Heriot Hill House with its entrance at the corner. A building which has made a plain statement of its unpretentious existence behind its circular carriage drive since 1788, it has two floors, and tripartite windows in a new frontage which, with the two short single-storey wings, were added shortly afterwards. Apart from featuring in the account, already given, of the meal-mob riots at Haig's Distillery, which must have taken place soon after it was built, no historical records seem to have survived of the house or its occupants. It has for many years been a Royal Navy and Royal Marine Club.

At the top of Scotland Street lies the beautiful and still comparatively quiet Drummond Place, built in the 1820s around the former Drummond Lodge, the mansionhouse of Lord Provost George Drummond (1687 - 1766), which then stood, facing Dublin Street, within the central gardens. On his death it had passed to General John Scott of Balcomie, when it was reconstructed under the altered name of Bellevue. And then, in 1802, it became the Excise Office, having been bought, believed Lord Cockburn, by the magistrates 'when the whole trees were instantly cut down.' He goes on nostalgically to 'remember people shuddering when they heard the axes busy in the woods of Bellevue, and furious when they saw the bare ground.' When the Scotland Street railway tunnel, which ran under Drummond Place, was built in 1842 it was decided to demolish the Excise Office because of the danger of subsidence.

The lands of Bellevue stretch eastwards from St Mary's Church. Just beyond Drummond Place and London Street (the latter originally called Anglia Street) is the former Catholic Apostolic Church completed in 1885 by Sir R. Rowand Anderson and containing mural paintings, considered today to be among the finest of their kind in Europe, by Dublin-born Mrs Phoebe Traquair (1852 - 1936), the first woman to be made an honorary member of the Royal Scottish Academy and a leader of the Edinburgh Arts and Crafts Movement, who commenced the work in 1893. The subjects include the parable of the Wise and Foolish Virgins, the Worship of Heaven from the Book of Revelation and the life of Christ, together with angel choirs and trumpeters, all moulded in relief and gilded. The cathedral-like interior has been used as a store and the murals are in a bad state of deterioration due very largely to water penetration from the roof. In March 1992 they became the subject of a statutory repair notice which was served on the owners, the Edinburgh Brick Company, the estimated cost of restoration being £19,000. By August 1993 this had risen to a figure between £600,000 and £900,000, including the cost of repair work to the building, as the damage had been greatly increased by torrential rain. An application had been received for the change of use of this place of worship to a night club, but, as strong opposition to this was widely expressed, the planning committee of Edinburgh District Council voted, in April 1992, to refuse permission. It is now to be hoped that a more appropriate use can be discovered for this splendid and prominently situated church building, and, although no purchaser has up till now been found, the interior has been upgraded, fund-raising for restoration is being undertaken and several proposals have been made for possible future use. The last Catholic Apostolic Service in the church took place in 1958.

To the east, and on the same side of East London Street as the church, is the Dutch-gabled Gayfield House built about 1765 in extensive grounds and now restricted within a street and behind a 'postage stamp' front garden. Built by Charles and William Butter, trading as wrights within the city, on land which had been feued from the Heriot Trust, the first owner was Thomas Erskine, son of the Earl of Mar, whose wife was Lady Charlotte Hope of the family that had built Hopetoun House at South Queensferry. Following his death in 1766 the mansion house passed to the 6th Earl of Leven. After further periods of private occupation Gayfield House became a veterinary college in 1874, set up, after a dispute, in deliberate opposition to the Royal Veterinary College, and so remained until 1904. Thereafter it served both commercial and residential purposes and, after several problems and setbacks had been overcome, it again became a family home and is now the object of sympathetic and gradual restoration. Interesting features within are the carved plaster ceiling in the drawing-room and the vigorous and well-preserved stencil decoration on the floors of the entrance hall and the upper landing. During ownership by the previous purchaser three original fireplaces were removed from the building, and replacements of the appropriate period are in course of being located and installed by the present, restoring, owners.

East Claremont Street is largely of 1820s vintage although gaps were not filled until long after that date. In the Ordnance Survey map of 1896, while the street has the same name as it has now, the houses on the eastern side, separated by the unfilled gaps, are marked 'Claremont Terrace.' And it was between Claremont Terrace and what later became Bellevue Road, on the land with its mansionhouse known as Broughton Park, that the Zoological Gardens—Edinburgh's first Zoo—were situated between the years, says Grant, '1840 to 1867' as a 'small imitation of the old Vauxhall Gardens in London.' It extended westwards only as far as Melgund Terrace. A marble works was at the top of Bellevue Place where the present Drummond School and playground were later sited, the reason for the school being built so far to the east of the main road being, it has been claimed, because of difficulties in obtaining firm ground for the foundations due to the presence here of one of the Bellevue sand pits already mentioned in connection with St Mary's Church.

At the Zoological Gardens, in addition to elephants, caged animals such as monkeys and tigers and even a bear in a bear-pit, soldiers from Edinburgh Castle enacted scenes from the Indian Mutiny and various military exploits, 'the fortifications and so forth being illuminated transparencies.' This early forerunner of the Edinburgh Festival Tattoo was not, apparently, a great success and 'two magnificent tigers sent from India' by the Marquess of Dalhousie, the Governor General at that time, were afterwards 'transmitted to the Zoological Gardens in London.' 'Here too', continues Grant, 'was Wood's Victoria Hall, a large timber-built edifice for musical entertainments, which was open till about 1857.'

During the period of its popularity 'the elephant', wrote D.P. Thomson in *By the Water of Leith*, 'was of course the favourite, carrying dozens of children about the grounds.' Although in 1844 it was able to announce that it was 'under Royal Patronage', by the 1860s disease was making 'havoc among its inmates, and despite widely publicised concerts, acrobatic performances, fireworks and illuminated displays by Montgolfier balloons . . . in the year 1867 Broughton Park had to close its doors and the ground was given over to the speculative builder; across it Bellevue Street was then laid out.

Near the foot of East Claremont Street, on the high ground above Broughton Road, stood Broughton Hall, the home of James Donaldson whose bequest funded the building of Donaldson's Hospital for deaf children, and just beyond, on the other, or southern, side, was Blandfield House behind its prominently located fountain on a site now occupied by Broughton Primary School (built in 1897) opposite the east end of Broughton Road, originally Lower Broughton Road. Round the corner, on the east side of McDonald Road, is Blandfield Cottage, now belonging to British Gas whose Edinburgh and South East District Office is nearby at No. 140 Broughton Road for which they have usurped the old name of Blandfield House. The double-gabled Blandfield Cottage has its original entrance, with a seventeenth century moulded doorway, on the north side.

Returning from this brief excursion beyond the eastern limits of Canonmills to the road which bears the name of Canonmills and leads downhill beside the high retaining wall of Heriot Hill House, the little opening is reached, at Munro Place, which gives access to a hidden row (though it can be seen from Canonmills Bridge) of recently restored and stone-cleaned Georgian flats, some of their rooms containing bed recesses.

At the foot of Munro Place were the byres of 'Auld' Dan Munro (hence the name) and from here his 'cow's milk' was taken daily to be sold in Canonmills and Inverleith. As butter was made on Fridays, there was always an ample supply of buttermilk to be had for the week-end. Duncan's byres succeeded those of Dan Munro and they had a shop in Warriston Place on the other side of the Water of Leith. Beside Duncan's dairy in this small area was Mr Scott's Laundry but this later, according to one account, became a *Daily Mail* paper store when that newspaper was produced on the Morrison & Gibb premises beyond the river.

A feature of Canonmills village life in the nineteenth century was the number of wives who augmented their husbands' earnings by acting as wet nurses and foster mothers, but as they tended to be the women whose health was suspect, or who were not strong enough to 'go out charring', this practice became prohibited. They lived in disreputable-looking buildings such as 'The Auld Hoose' and 'The Happy Land', as two of them came to be called.

In his book *Parliament House—A Short History and Guide*, The Hon. Lord Cullen sheds a little further light on the life of the village women. 'From the 1740s until practically the end of the century', he writes, 'part of the area at the north end of the Hall was partitioned off for the use of the Bailie Court. According to Robert Chambers, this was popularly known as the "dirt court" as it was "chiefly resorted to by the washerwomen from Canonmills and the drunken alewives of the Canongate".'

A health hazard was the Water of Leith itself which was rat-infested. In winter, when snow and ice prevented them from finding food, they entered shops and houses and, like a plague of locusts, devoured the supplies that should have fed the villagers. The whole district, with its orchards and fields of strawberries, continued to have a rural, village character until the mid-nineteenth century, and this is summed up well in a popular verse, or jingle, of the time:

Canonmills
Where young folks gang to get their fills
Of curds and cream, and fine gooseberries,
Apples, pears and geans and cherries.

At the top of Munro Place stands a little building containing a hall and other ancillary accommodation. And it was in this hall that a very small Robert Louis Stevenson first went to school, although the appearance of the building, which was remodelled in 1906, has changed since then. This was one of Edinburgh's 'penny schools' where pupils of seven and under were taught for one penny a week; 2d was charged for children over seven. The building later became the Youth Centre of Dublin Street Baptist Church when a plaque was placed on the outside wall, next to Munro Place, depicting a head of Stevenson between the dates 1850 and 1894, which represent his foreshortened lifespan, with the inscription underneath: *In this Hall Robert Louis Stevenson first went to school circa 1857.* He had been born across the river at No. 8 Howard Place and had then moved with his family to No. 1 Inverleith Terrace. The plaque was designed by a member of the congregation, Tom Curr, M.B.E., J.P., an Edinburgh bailie. Mr Curr, who lived in East Claremont Street, was well-known as a cartoonist

A bronze head of Robert Louis Stevenson on the south wall of Canonmills Baptist Church indicates the hall in which he first attended school.

with the *Edinburgh Evening News* and also for his work with the Boys' Brigade in this hall where he was captain of the 46th Company. It had been launched here at Canonmills in 1903 and, although it was disbanded in 1923, it was revived under Mr Curr and went on to become the largest company in the Edinburgh Battalion. The poetry written by his wife, Christian Curr, was published in the 1930s and '40s and her book *Queen's Shores and Other Verses*, with a foreword by the Lord Provost Sir William Y. Darling and illustrated by her husband, was brought out by Oliver and Boyd in 1943.

The congregation which became Dublin Street Baptist Church was formed in 1810 in Laing's Academy in East Thistle Street and moved, in 1813, to Elder Street where they remained till increasing numbers necessitated the building of a larger place of worship. The new church was erected, on the site of a cabinet-maker's workshop, in Dublin Street and was completed in 1858. One hundred and thirty years later, when major structural repairs became essential, a decision was taken to remove once more, but this time it proved possible to utilise the premises which they already owned in Canonmills. Robert Louis Stevenson's old school had been in their possession since 1885 when it had served as a mission station for the congregation. After the adaptation of the Hall into a multi-purpose church the congregation, in the fourth removal in its history, held its first service here in October 1988 under its new name of Canonmills Baptist Church. It is of considerable interest that a Baptist church should be located here in close proximity to that part of the Water of Leith where, as the brief history of the congregation prepared when they came downhill from Dublin Street observes, 'more than two centuries ago, services of believers' baptism were held.' The additional rooms within this building are now in constant use as this small but significant congregation carries out its work and witness—relating 'the whole of life to the Christian

A Scots-Baronial tenement of 1863 at the top of Warriston Road in the heart of Canonmills.

Faith'—beside the busy crossroads junction at Canonmills Bridge. The church in Dublin Street was demolished and has been replaced by a Georgian-style development of city centre office accommodation.

The church stands in the street called Canonmills which curves round the corner to a baker's shop (now Taylor, but previously Notman and before that Dunbar) and the top of Warriston Road. Redevelopment is planned for the disused buildings (which belonged to McGlashen, the monumental sculptors, who will be mentioned later) between the church and the shop, directly opposite Canonmills Service Station with its old Baxters' lintel of 1686, but the Warriston Road corner terminates the street with a fine Victorian flourish. A Scots-Baronial tenement, complete with crowsteps and corbelled turret, was built here in 1863, a stone's throw from the Water of Leith at 'Puddocky'.

CHAPTER 4

The Bridge and the River

I have remarked upon the surprising sense of inadequacy that the Water of Leith gives, seen as the watercourse of a great city. It comes into Edinburgh by chance, having had nothing to do with the foundation of the City and only being incorporated late in its history. It is a burn, in fact, a trickle of hill water running twenty miles from its source in the Pentland Hills to the harbour of Leith. It is even sometimes disrespectfully referred to as the Puddocky Burn by the small boys who splash and paddle in its shallows by Canonmills, and catch reidbreisters and mennans [minnows], and the trout fry occasionally put down in the water by an optimistic Corporation. In the old days it must have been, for its size, one of the busiest waters in the world. Along less than twenty miles there were seventy mills: in places so close together that there was only a six-inch fall between one lade and the next. Wheat-flour and oatmeal were milled for the provision of Edinburgh, and latterly snuff-milling was quite an important ploy. The last of Leith Water's snuff mills was closed down during the late war on the death of its jolly miller, the worthy Mr Walker who played on his fiddle while the wheels turned and pulverised the tobacco leaves. There are still a few mills, and the Water sluices a tannery at the Dean, and does some other menial tasks as it passes through Edinburgh.

So wrote the late George Scott-Moncrieff in 1947, two years after the end of the Second World War, but the scene he paints has changed during the subsequent forty-five years. Other mills besides the snuff mill have been closed and there is no longer a tannery at the Dean. But

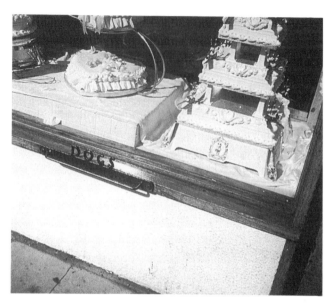

How many years have passed since dogs were tied up at this little dog-rail outside the Bakers' shop, on the ground floor of the Baronial tenement, while their owners were inside?

the 'trickle of hill water', which starts above Harperrigg Reservoir, is still flowing, covering a distance of thirty-five kilometres (twenty-three miles) to the sea at Leith. The compensation pond of Harperrigg was built across the watercourse to provide additional water-power for downstream industries, and some of the springs which feed the river have from time to time been diverted for similar purposes.

The Water of Leith enters the city from the Pentland Hills, flowing into and out of Harperrigg Reservoir, by way of Balerno, Currie, Juniper Green, Colinton, Slateford, Saughton, Gorgie, Roseburn, beneath Coltbridge and Belford Bridge, the Dean Village and Stockbridge. From here it runs by the sylvan Rocheid Path, with its little rustic bridge, behind the Stockbridge Colonies to flow Leithwards under Canonmills Bridge where, at 'Puddocky', it has always been wadeable except when in spate. Its journey continues by the north side of Warriston Road to Redbraes, then to Bonnington, under Great Junction Street, past The Shore and into the Harbour beside Leith Docks.

There was a ford at Canonmills from time immemorial and, when the building of houses began in Inverleith and Trinity, the river, which could run (as indeed, on occasion, it still can) high and brown with floodwater from its source among the heather, was an obstacle to easy and rapid progress towards these areas. Under normal conditions it had to be crossed on foot or on horseback. The solution was a bridge at this shallow, fordable point and the first bridge, a single, stone, humpbacked span, was built in 1761, providing quick and convenient access to the north for horse-drawn carriages and all wheeled traffic. As the nineteenth century advanced a larger and more substantial bridge became necessary and it was replaced by a three-arch structure in 1840. Its width was increased in 1896 and it is this bridge which spans the 'Leith Water' at the present day and on which can be read, on the eastern side, the inscription:

Bridge built 1840
Widened 1896
The Right-Hon.
Andrew McDonald
Lord Provost
David C. Proudfoot
Engineer

In Brandon Terrace space was allocated for a cab rank and here also the horses whose job it was to pull the omnibuses from Trinity to The Mound were fed from tubs of meal and watered, the water being obtained from a metal feature in the shape of a round pillar which stood on the east side of the Drill Hall about a hundred yards west of the bridge. A door in the 'pillar' could be opened to reveal a pail from which the horses drank. These wells were often accompanied by a cabmen's shelter which had the appearance of a cabin raised on stilts and which was approached by two or three steps leading up to the door. Such shelters, of varying sizes, could be found throughout the city.

Prior to the introduction of cab ranks there had been a stance for sedan chairs at the north end of the bridge manned by four chairmen and four porters who had been taken into employment at this point as a consequence of a petition from the residents in Warriston Crescent, Howard Place and Inverleith Row who did not own carriages and who therefore required their services when 'venturing forth of an evening to the ball or the theatre.' One account suggests that the duties of chairmen and porters were interchangeable and that each was equipped with at least 'four fathoms' of rope and two creels, one for coal and the other for bottles, so that, when not carrying chairs, these jacks-of-all-trades became coal and bottle hauliers and were no doubt thankful enough, if this was so, thus to supplement their remuneration.

Sedan chairs were used widely in the Old Town where, in the wynds and closes, they were the most efficient form of transport, and were carried by stalwart Highlanders, the survivors of the Jacobite wars who had come to Edinburgh seeking employment. Hackney-sedans were in continual demand by the 1730s (though the sedan chair had been introduced as early as the late 1660s), their wooden framework covered with canvas and black leather contrasting with those that were privately owned which were usually colourful and often richly decorated. They had a door at the front but the

roof was hinged and could be lifted up for greater con-
venience when entering or leaving. The carrying poles
passed through rings on either side of the chair. These
picturesque conveyances were seldom used by people
below the status of the professional classes and, on their
removal to the New Town towards the end of the eighteenth century, the sedans and the chairmen went with
them and they were still in use well into the 1850s in
spite of the spacious new streets so admirably suited to
horses and carriages. The round badge of the Society of
Chairmen showed, in the centre, a chair being carried
by two of their number, a border containing their motto
Honesty is the Best Policy and, at the top, a crown and
the date. A table of fares for Hackney-chairs was drawn
up and, in 1810, they could be hired for a whole day
(10 a.m. to midnight) for 7/6d (38p) or from 9 a.m. to
4 p.m. for 3/6d (18p). The last sedan chair for hire in
Edinburgh stood at the corner of Great King Street and
Dundas Street till about 1870.

Buildings, now gone, beside the bridge on the western
side were the Drill Hall on the north side of Brandon
Terrace (No. 31) and the toll-house. The Drill Hall of
the 528th (Lowland) Ammunition Company R.A.S.C. was
for many years used for other purposes, the last occupants being Rentokil. It was demolished in 1991 by The
Standard Life Assurance Company after serving as a site
office during the construction of their new offices at Tanfield. The white-washed, slate-roofed toll-house or 'Brig
Toll' stood at the south-west corner of the bridge, at the
point subsequently occupied by the recently rebuilt public
conveniences, and was demolished in 1896 when the
bridge was widened.

The stream flowing under Canonmills Bridge, was, and
remains, one of the five principal rivers of Lothian—the
Tyne, the Esk, the Water of Leith, the Almond and—the
longest—the Avon. Anglers catch fish in it (it is stocked
annually with trout), its waters have been polluted and

A View of Edinburgh from Canonmills by John Knox (1778 -
1845). This picture, showing the original single-arched Canonmills
Bridge and women bleaching linen by the Water of Leith, was
painted shortly before the builders of the New Town reached
Canonmills. (Photograph courtesy The National Gallery of Scotland)

purified by turns, books have been written about it and
its beauties and attractions have been praised in verse and
song. Even the much-derided McGonagall has contributed
to its literature with *The River of Leith*:

> Therefore all lovers of the picturesque be advised by me
> And the beautiful scenery of the River of Leith go and see,
> And I am sure you will get a very great treat,
> Because the River of Leith scenery cannot be beat.

An apposite footnote is appended to these lines in *The
Water of Leith* edited by Stanley Jamieson for The Water
of Leith Project Group:

The poet will be forgiven his failure to give the river its correct name, in consideration of the soundness of his advice and the warmth of his encomium!

But more in line with the great traditions of Scottish poetry is *To the Water o'Leith* in *Rhymes o' Auld Reekie* by Douglas Fraser who captures the mood of 'the trickle of hill water' when it becomes a torrent:

> But, trith to tell, although ye're fine
> Ye're no' the Tiber or the Rhine;
> Ye're kinna blate
> Until the snaws on Pentlands melt
> When broun and swirlin' doun ye pelt
> In muckle spate.

Like the other Lothian rivers, the Leith Water has its own flora and fauna. One of the most attractive plants is the Indian Balsam with its pink, orchid-like flowers, an incomer among the native wild flowers which has become well established in the Stockbridge/Canonmills/Warriston stretch of the river. Also to be found, and to be carefully avoided, are the poisonous sow-thistle and deadly nightshade, as well as a variety of grasses. A serious problem in recent times has been the giant hogweed, not so life-threatening as those just mentioned but nevertheless injurious if contact is made with its sap. A member of the *umbillifer* family and a relation of the humble cow parsley, it was introduced from the Russian Caucasus as a large ornamental exotic into Victorian gardens from which it escaped to spread outwards to cemeteries and waterways for which it has a particular preference. Its tall stems, huge leaves and white 'flower umbrellas' keep sunlight from the neighbouring vegetation and erode the riverbanks. Attempts to combat this persistent intruder have been made by Lothian District Council and at Warriston Road the solution has been to cover part of its ground-area with concrete.

Like Canonmills Loch of old, the river provides a natural habitat for birds and mammals, coot, common tern, blackbird, thrush, house sparrow and blackheaded gull among the former. The Water of Leith is also graced with swans, but to see them it is necessary to go downstream to The Shore where, before the closure of the lock gates at the Docks in 1969, the river used to be tidal and a feeding habitat for a wide variety of birds. The decline of the mute swan in the British Isles has resulted in the loss of their nests from the riverbanks at places such as Roseburn, Warriston and Leith, though it is at least a possibility that they may perhaps become re-established. Badgers, mainly nocturnal animals, have their setts by the Water and voles and stoats are abundant, providing food for the foraging owls and the numerous foxes which come out at night from their holes in Warriston Cemetery. Urban foxes have become increasingly common in the recent past.

The city has for some years been creating walkways by the river and the riverside path at Canonmills can be reached from the east end of Warriston Crescent. From here it follows the disused railway line by way of the cemetery and Bonnington and emerges at the former Junction Bridge Railway Depot, now called Coalie Park, in North Leith. The Depot was acquired in 1968 from British Rail, and the railway line to Warriston in 1980.

The streets which converge at or near the top of Warriston Road are Brandon Terrace, The B-listed Huntly Street, Canon Lane, Canon Street, Canonmills (leading down from Rodney Street), Warriston Road itself and, at the age-old crossing of the Water of Leith, Canonmills Bridge. This area comprises the heart of present-day

The Canonmills Clock with, behind, offices of The Standard Life Assurance Company opened by the Queen in 1991.

Canonmills. Towards the eastern end of Brandon Terrace stands the Canonmills Clock presented in 1945 by Archibald G. Bryson, C.A. (1873 - 1959). Mr Bryson, Session Clerk of St Mary's Parish Church in Bellevue Crescent from 1917 to 1938, had for long felt the need for a clock in this area and his gift was made in commemoration of the Allied victory in the Second World War and in gratitude for the safe return of his own sons. The four-dial clock within a bronze metal case and on an Art Deco pedestal was designed by L. Grahame Thomson, R.S.A., F.R.I.B.A., and the movement was provided by James Ritchie & Sons, the famous Edinburgh watch- and clock-makers, then in Leith Street and now in Broughton Street. This clock was moved a few feet to the west when the Standard Life Assurance Company building was being constructed on the other side of the river and the original position is now marked by a raised arrangement of setts in the road which acts as a small traffic roundabout. This original position of the clock was, of old, occupied by a round island with a tall street lamp in the middle of it.

In Warriston Road, a short distance east of the baronial tenement on the corner, Warriston Farm Cottage has survived many changes in its immediate surroundings, the one exception being the Water of Leith which still flows on ignoring the fluctuating fortunes of the little cottage. Starting life in the late eighteenth century with, as now, whitewashed walls and a red pantiled roof, this was a farm cottage rather than a farmhouse and would stand amid a small farmyard with such animals as a cow or two, a goat and a few pigs and hens.

The mid-nineteenth century brought the first changes with the arrival of the railway and Heriothill Station, when the cottage became the station gatehouse, and the building of the now disused railway bridge for the Edinburgh, Leith and Newhaven Railway which was completed in 1843. Spanning the road as well as the river, this substantial structure consists of three arches supported on well buttressed cutwaters by Grainger & Miller who had been responsible for the sea wall at Newhaven in 1837 and were to design North Leith Station in 1846.

In another change of role the cottage then became the home of a 'mussel boiler' who departed some time later leaving it littered with mussel shells. After falling into near-dereliction, it was rescued in more recent times by Janet Adam who converted it into her Canonmills Pottery, with a kiln chimney attached to the eastern gable, for which it was admirably suited. But she was forced to leave when the Lothian Chemical Co. Ltd., whose entrance was at No. 3 Broughton Road, sold their site between Warriston Road and Broughton Road for housebuilding purposes in 1982 to re-establish their operations at West Shore Road at Granton. The cottage then became the site office for Leech Homes, the homes springing up with the rapidity of the prophet's gourd once the ground had been cleared. The potter had traced and written the history of the cottage and this interesting document was posted up on one of the walls where it could be read while admiring the ceramics displayed on the shelves. She had also recreated the cottage garden at the back but this, of course, has vanished. While larger and better-known houses are disappearing from the Edinburgh streets, Warriston Farm Cottage has survived and, restored and with a short addition at the western end, it is again in non-residential use as a photographic processing laboratory.

The short row of tenements here was for long called Catherine Place until incorporated into Warriston Road and the old name can still be read on the walls.

The name given to the new housing development by Leech Homes is Boat Green. In spite of its proximity to

The Water of Leith from Canonmills Bridge. The low, whitewashed walls and red-pantiled roof of the former Warriston Farm Cottage can be seen on the right bank.

the once navigable Water of Leith, this has no connection with boats. It is a corruption of 'Booths'. On old maps of the district this ground has the appearance of a bleaching green and in a deed of 1759 it is referred to as 'Booths Green'. It may therefore be reasonable to conclude that someone called Booth was responsible for a laundry and bleaching green here either at that time or at an earlier date. It was part of this land that later became the railway goods station called Heriothill. Booths Green Cottage is shown eastwards of Warriston Farm Cottage (which is not shown) on Johnston's Plan of Edinburgh and Leith of 1851. It disappeared many years ago.

A short distance to the south-west of Warriston Farm Cottage a small ruinous building, which may have been a cottage, and which will no doubt shortly be dispensed with, was exposed by the demolition, completed in May 1993, of the disused McGlashen workshop (referred to below) where a new building fronting Canonmills, to be called Canonmills House, is to be built on this site. And on ground behind Warriston Farm Cottage is an erstwhile house with a tall, pointed gable having ball finials on either side of the base and an adjacent window surmounted by a gablet, all facing west. On the south side, facing a small car park, are two windows (the eastern one blocked up) with gablets above each window. Industrial buildings belonging to Mackinnon & Hay Ltd., Polythene Bag Manufacturers at No. 3 Warriston Road, are joined to it on the west and east sides, the west-facing gable and window being visible above them; they can also now be seen by looking down Warriston Road from Huntly Street.

Beyond the railway bridge, at No. 9 Warriston Road, are the red sandstone Office and Show Rooms of Lady Haig's Poppy Factory by A. Hunter Crawford, of the well-known family of bakers, whose most important work was the Freemasons's Hall in George Street. The offices, and factory behind them, had belonged to McLagan &

Cumming Ltd., the fine-art Lithographic printers, who moved to Warriston Road in 1891. The late Tom Curr, already mentioned in connection with Canonmills Baptist Church, was a director of this firm. Amalgamating with McCorquodale of Glasgow, they vacated their Warriston Road premises, which then became a Cash and Carry Warehouse, in 1964.

The Poppy Factory had been established in 1938 in Tolbooth Wynd, Calton Road, and moved to No. 129 Canongate in 1949 where they remained until their last removal, to Warriston Road, in 1968 at which date they also had a shop in George Street. The premises in Warriston Road then became The Earl Haig Fund (Scotland) H.Q. and now, as New Haig House, entered from Logie Green Road, they also contain the Royal British Legion Scotland National Headquarters. In its earlier years the Poppy Factory gave employment only to badly disabled First World War ex-servicemen, this being one of the reasons for its establishment, but the only requirement for employment now is disability due to any cause.

A. Hunter Crawford was also responsible for the red sandstone building at the opposite corner of Logie Green Road and Warriston Road occupied by the works of George Waterston & Sons Ltd., the printers and stationers of George Street. In addition to their own stationery, bank notes were printed here until recent times. And for a large part of the present century the Beaverhall Works of Thos. Symington & Co. Ltd., manufacturers of coffee essence, were at No. 65 Logie Green Road.

The North British Marble Works were situated at the top of Glenogle Road and a sculptors' and stone-cutters' yard, which continued their work, was subsequently set up beside Canonmills Bridge. It was here that Stewart McGlashen, the monumental sculptors, were in operation for many years. The building (now demolished as already stated) between the bakers' shop and what is now

Canonmills Baptist Church belonged to them and was where most of their work was carried on, although there was a small area nearer the riverbank, on the other side of Warriston Road behind their shop premises on the bridge, which was also used. The sculptor Stewart McGlashen, who died in 1904, is known to have carved at least one of the West Highland crosses in Warriston Cemetery, probably in 1871, and his firm, Stewart McGlashen & Son, established as early as 1836, was responsible for the Celtic Cross commemorating the Scottish Horse on the Castle Esplanade in 1905. Later becoming a limited company, they described themselves as architectural craftsmen in granite and stone who also undertook church decoration and installed 'shopfronts etc.'.

When London Bridge, commenced in 1825 by the Scots-born engineer Sir John Rennie, was being demolished, some of the Craigleith stone from the bridge approach was bought by Stewart McGlashen & Son of Canonmills with the intention that it should be used in the making of gravestones. The bridge had been purchased (under the mistaken impression, it was said, that it was Tower Bridge) by an American company who shipped it across the Atlantic and re-erected it, where it now is, in the Nevada Desert. But the stone bought by McGlashen and brought back to Edinburgh did not end up in a cemetery. When the ground-floor and basement of Nos. 127 - 129 George Street were being refaced during the years 1973 - 75 by the architects Robert Hurd & Partners, it was the old London Bridge stone that proved to be the only Craigleith stone that was available (the old worked-out quarry having been some years ago filled in) and which is now incorporated in these George Street buildings then being reconstructed for a branch of the Bank of Chicago which has since departed. Only the facade, all of it still built of native Craigleith stone, now survives. The stone-masons Stewart McGlashen are still in business but are no longer based in Edinburgh.

When, in 1842, Queen Victoria paid her first visit to Edinburgh after her coronation, it was to have been at Brandon Street that the ceremony of the presentation of the keys of the city was to have taken place, and for this royal occasion a triumphal arch was erected beneath which it had been arranged for the procession to halt when the Queen's carriage had reached this point. The story is well-known, however, of the overturning of these plans by what would today be called a breakdown in communications. Sir James Forrest, who was Lord Provost of Edinburgh at the time, was under a misapprehension regarding the time of arrival at Granton of the Royal Yacht. But Provost James Reoch of Leith had been alerted and it was he and the bailies of the Port who were promptly and proudly on hand to welcome the Queen and Prince Albert instead of the tardy James Forrest and the Edinburgh magistrates.

In the confusion which followed, the dense crowds at Canonmills Bridge and in Brandon Terrace, who had gathered in spite of the early hour (it was 6 a.m.) at which the Queen had disembarked on the morning of September first, were amazed to see the whole procession sweep through the archway without stopping, while, coming hell for leather from the opposite direction, the Royal Company of Archers, the Queen's bodyguard in Scotland, made a frenzied effort to reach the scene before it was too late. One of their number, Lord Elcho, was nearly thrown under the royal carriage wheels. The young Queen is said to have laughed merrily at the results of this civic blundering and to have driven straight on to Dalkeith Palace where she was to stay. Greater planning precision ensured more orderly arrangements on her later official entry into the city.

In time-honoured fashion, the citizenry of Edinburgh put the matter succinctly in doggerel verse composed in parody of the old Jacobite words, and sung to the old tune, of *Hey, Johnnie Cope*:

Hey Jamie Forrest are ye waukin' yet?
Or are your Bailies snorin' yet?
If ye are waukin' I would wit
Ye'd hae a merry, merry mornin'!
The Queen she's come to Granton pier,
Nae Provost and nae Bailies here:
They're in their beds I muckle fear
Sae early in the mornin':
The Queen she's come to Brandon Street,
The Provost and the keys to meet,
An' div ye think that she's to wait
Ye're waukin' in the mornin'!

Sir James Forrest of Comiston (1780 - 1860) was an excellent Lord Provost and it is regrettable that he is remembered more for this unfortunate episode than for his many public services to the City of Edinburgh.

CHAPTER 5

Tanfield

The triangular site, in the valley of the Water of Leith, adjacent to Canonmills Bridge which has recently been extensively redeveloped by The Standard Life Assurance Company has been known as Tanfield for generations in consequence of a tanyard set up on the riverbank. At a later date (probably in the eighteenth century) Tanfield House was built at the north-west side of the triangle, but no trace of this has existed for some considerable time. It was not until the 'peculiar edifice' in the shape of a Moorish fortress was erected, in 1825, at the southern side on the north bank of the Water of Leith that the area acquired some significance in the history of Edinburgh. This was an oil-gas works (gas lighting had been invented in 1792 by a Scotsman called William Murdoch), the imaginative brainchild of the Oil Gas Co. and William Burn, the prominent nineteenth century Edinburgh architect whom they commissioned to design it. The chairman of the company was Sir Walter Scott by whom the foundation stone had been laid in 1824. Westwards of this structure the Portable Gas Works was built at much the same time and there appears to have been a good deal of rivalry between the two gas companies. (The only other gas company of significance in Edinburgh was The Gaslight Company noted, after 1849, for its high chimney, in New Street in the Old Town.)

The attempts made by the Oil Gas Co. to manufacture gas from whale oil were unsuccessful but their failure may have been partly due to the proximity of the rival company. At all events the Oil Gas Co. was closed in 1839 when the retort houses in the 'Moorish fortress' became the Tanfield Hall, a building which achieved

Tanfield Hall from the foot of Brandon Street (from *Old and New Edinburgh* by James Grant)

immediate and enduring fame when the Free Church of Scotland was inaugurated here at the Disruption in 1843. It is, however, recorded by Grant and other historians that in 1835 a banquet was held in the Hall in honour of the Irish patriot and liberal MP, Daniel O'Connell. The Disruption was the last and most devastating of the many secessions from the Church of Scotland which took place during the eighteenth and early nineteenth centuries, largely on account of what was seen as the evils of patronage - the denial of a congregation's right to call a minister of its own choice to a vacant charge, the appointee being imposed instead by the heritor or landowner. This undesirable practice was the result of the 1712 Act of Patronage and the fact that the heritors had been responsible for providing and maintaining parish churches and manses and also for payment of ministers' stipends. The whole question of the relationship between Church and State was involved, and the undertaking given in the Revolution Settlement of 1690 (by which Presbyterianism was officially established within Scotland) that the Scottish church should be wholly independent ought to have prevented the passing of the Act of 1712. Patronage was officially abolished in 1874 and the seceders began gradually to 'heal the breach' with the parent church, culminating in the final reunion of 1929.

A 'great schism' was expected to take place when the General Assembly of the Church of Scotland met in St Andrew's (now St Andrew's and St George's) Church in George Street on 18 May 1843, although there were those who believed that 'a mere few would relinquish their comfortable stipends and their pleasant manses' for the sake of their principles. Dr Welsh, the Moderator, read a formal protest, which had been signed by 120 'Non-intrusion' ministers and 72 elders, and then took the initiative by walking out of the building. Closely followed by Dr Thomas Chalmers and some others, he took the road (Hanover Street) which led downhill from George Street to Canonmills. Soon they were joined by many more until 474 men 'poured forth along the streets' to many indications of approval from the gathered crowd of onlookers. Shaking the dust of the establishment from their feet, they proceeded 'to cross their Rubicon' at the Water of Leith and then at Tanfield Hall, in accordance with arrangements which had been made in anticipation of this outcome of events, they constituted themselves the General Assembly of the Free Church of Scotland and appointed Thomas Chalmers, DD, as their first Moderator.

The historic scene at Tanfield was subsequently painted by the artist and pioneer photographer David Octavius Hill, RSA, (who had lived in Inverleith Row before removing to Rock House on the Calton Hill) in a huge canvas which now hangs in the Presbytery Hall of the Free Church Offices at The Mound. In preparation for this work, which took him twenty-three years to complete, he and his associate, Robert Adamson, photographed every person present in order that each one would be represented by an accurate portrait. Standing prominently at the front is Hugh Miller, the Cromarty stonemason, famous geologist, author, and first editor of *The Witness*, the newspaper, or periodical, of the Free Church.

Canonmills saw these dramatic events in the year following the visit of the young Queen Victoria, when the stark contrast in mood and circumstances would not be lost on anyone who was present on both occasions.

Four years later, in 1847, Tanfield Hall was also the scene of another, and happier, event in the annals of the church in Scotland. This was the union between the Relief and the Secession Churches (the latter having already formed a union themselves) which created the United Presbyterian Church of Scotland - usually referred to as the UPs.

The Portable Gas Company continued its operations until the 1930s, acquiring ground on the south side of the river on the site where the Croall and Croall Garages (with, latterly, their neon car advertisement signs) were built in 1965, but the Oil Gas Co.'s buildings were altered and partially dismantled in the course of time. The 'Moorish' structure was cruciform in plan but only one of the four 'arms' survived until the final clearance of the site by the Standard Life. In the early years of the twentieth century, long before Croall and Croall's day, a cottage laundry and bleaching green, called the Heriot Laundry, was situated on the opposite corner of Glenogle Road. An area of grass can be seen on the north side of the former R. & R. Clark facade and the iron gate in the railings is still there, all that remains of the laundry premises.

During the period when the streets of Edinburgh were lit by gas, Gasholder No. 1 was positioned here on the

north bank of the Water of Leith. Owned by a private
concern, Tanfield Gas Station was later taken over by the
Edinburgh Corporation Gas Company who continued to
provide gas for street lighting until the large Granton Gas
Works, designed by W.R. Herring for the Edinburgh and
Leith Corporation Gas Commissioners, was built and
brought into operation in 1906.

Five circular gasholders were situated in the triangular
area behind the woolstore (to be mentioned later) and
three on the south side of the Water of Leith. To contain
them pits of similar shape were dug in the ground and
partly filled with water so that, when full of gas, the
holders rose, and then sank as they were emptied. An
edging of sandstone blocks was visible round the top of
each pit and when excavation was taking place in Glenogle Road for the Standard Life Assurance Company the
pit walls could be seen for a short time prior to their
demolition. The five northerly pits had been filled in with
domestic rubbish before Morrison & Gibb built their
western extension over them in 1937.

At the foot of Tanfield Lane a back lane, on the other
side of which the Morrison & Gibb extension was afterwards laid out, ran north and south and at its southern
end stood Gas Works House. Built to house the employees, it was constructed on the same lines as those in the
nearby Stockbridge Colonies and consisted of two flats,
the upper being approached by a long flight of steps. Gas
Works House was still in occupation when the site was
purchased by Standard Life who made the necessary
rehousing arrangements.

The Morrison & Gibb connection with Tanfield (a site
which, as can be seen, supports several layers of history)
began when they acquired part of this area to set up
their printing and bookbinding works on the north side
of Tanfield Lane which ran between them and the gas
works. They built a low red sandstone range, fronting
the short street known as Tanfield opposite Howard

A plan of the Morrison & Gibb complex of buildings c. 1938. At the extreme left are the circular gasholder pits between which and the Tanfield buildings runs the Water of Leith. At top right are the light-coloured roofs of the Morrison & Gibb Western Extension with Gas Works House at its southern end. The 1896 Morrison & Gibb red sandstone range is at the bottom with Tanfield Lane on its left and the former woolstore at an oblique angle behind. Across the lane from the woolstore is the one remaining section of the former Tanfield Hall. After demolition this area became the site of new offices for The Standard Life Assurance Company and only the facade of the woolstore now remains.

Place, in 1896. The architect was Robert Wilson who also designed a number of schools in the city. Behind this new building a former three-storey woolstore with three gablets at roof level, standing at an oblique angle to the 1896 range, probably dates from c. 1865. (It has been claimed that it was built at this angle because it was originally intended that the road from Dundas Street and

Pitt Street should turn the corner by running directly in front of it, but there are maps which, although showing the intended line of the road, do not indicate the presence of any building at this point.) Prior to 1860 a wool-broker called Robert Girdwood had premises on the Tanfield Hall side of Tanfield Lane and appears to have expanded to the other side of the lane about seven years later.

The large extension on the western side gave the company, to quote its advertisements, 'almost two acres of manufacturing floor space laid out with a view to increased efficiency in all departments' which were 'equipped with special plant to meet the demands of Modern Publicity and mark the opening of our second century of progressive printing practice.'

After the Second World War the *Daily Mail* newspaper started production of a Scottish version - the *Scottish Daily Mail*. For this purpose premises were leased from Morrison & Gibb and it was printed, during the night, at Tanfield by the paper's own printing staff from 1st December 1948 until 30 November 1968 - a period of exactly twenty years. Their editorial department occupied the top floor of the woolstore, the floor below being the caseroom where the type was set. The basement of this building and the Tanfield Hall 'arm' became paper stores.

At the beginning of 1982 the assets and stock of Morrison & Gibb were purchased by another company, Clark Constable, who rescued them from receivership, but they were again in the hands of a receiver six months later and the Tanfield buildings were closed in July of that year. They had employed about three hundred workers.

The buildings on the north side of Tanfield Lane which represented all that remained of the Portable Gas Works were for many years a bonded warehouse for the whisky distillers, Macdonald & Muir Ltd. of Leith.

On 26 February 1986 a planning application by The Standard Life Assurance Company of George Street, the European Community's largest mutual life company, for the demolition of the former printing works of Morrison & Gibb, the former bonded warehouse of Macdonald & Muir and the few remains of Tanfield Hall was lodged with Edinburgh District Council. The company's plans were to build a £30 million (the final cost was to be £45 million) Administrative Office and Data Centre on the site to be designed by the architects The Michael Laird Partnership. After considering a move to the out-skirts of Edinburgh at South Gyle, and having already built new premises in Annandale Street on the north side of the city, the site at Tanfield was chosen because it was situated at a convenient distance from their other premises in George Street, Thistle Street and Annandale Street. The result has been a transformation of the whole layout around Canonmills Bridge. The former drill hall in Brandon Terrace, used as a site office during building op-erations, was demolished and the riverbank on the southern side was then landscaped and planted with trees.

The Tanfield ground was found to contain a certain amount of pollution from both the gas companies' oper-ations and the printing works, and special measures had to be taken to dispose of it. In addition, it was necessary to divert the course of a vital underground gas main, supplying gas to Edinburgh's South Side, to the former Croall and Croall site on the southern bank of the river. Only after these problems had been overcome could building work on the project be commenced.

An innovative modern structure covering some 20,000 square metres of office space had been designed by the architects, each floor of the main building at Tanfield House having total floor space equivalent to the size of the Murrayfield rugby ground. Located in the Water of Leith valley, the low-lying buildings are surmounted by three domes fitted with photo-electric cells which control solar blinds under the glass, thereby giving automatic pro-tection from the sun to all staff working at Visual Display Unit terminals. Underneath the domes are three circular, landscaped atria, and, at dome level, is a roof-top restaurant from which access is obtainable to a landscaped roof-garden with panoramic views across the city. The main entrance is approached across a piazza from Tanfield/Howard Place and leads to an opulent main staircase worthy of a Medici palace.

The former woolstore was demolished with the exception of the south-east wall (its retention was an excellent decision) behind which has been built the coffee lounge and here, in accordance with their practice of giving encouragement to contemporary Scottish painters, seven large panels are displayed on the walls. The work of the Edinburgh artist Andrew Smith, they depict scenes in the city at different times of day from dawn to dusk. On the south side of the Water of Leith is the Data Centre, car parking facilities are located in the basement of the main building and a new bridge has been built across the river from the top of Glenogle Road where several structures, including the Croall and Croall Garages and a warehouse belonging to James Gray & Son of No. 89 George Street, were demolished. A row of stone ball finials can be seen above the riverbank on the north side. These were formerly ornamental features on the wallhead of a warehouse at this point and have, happily, also been retained and augmented by several reproductions. The final alteration on the south side of the Water of Leith was the removal of the Bryson clock a few feet to the west and the creation of the small traffic roundabout at its former position.

To the east the tenements and shops at Howard Street remain on the south-east corner of the Standard Life property, but a few single-storey buildings occupied as shops were demolished to make way for the northern entrance gates.

Within the southern entrance gates of Tanfield House stands a twenty-feet high black granite obelisk bearing the words *Axis Mundi* and supporting a group of five winged figures representing the ascent of or the *Apotheosis of the Wise Virgins* which is the alternative title of this graceful work, dated 1991, by the sculptor Gerald Ogilvie Laing. No stranger to the Standard Life Assurance Company, he was commissioned by them to create, in relief, a bronze frieze on the same New Testament theme to adorn the wallhead of the George Street extension of their original building on the corner of that street and St Andrew Square. The frieze was placed here in 1980. The 'wise virgins' had in fact appeared initially within the pediment of their St Andrew Square offices when first built in the 1890s, the sculptor at that time being Sir John Steell.

Sundials can also be seen on the south, west and east sides of the *Axis Mundi* obelisk, and on the west face of the tip of the obelisk is a palindrome which it is possible to read upwards or downwards and backwards or forwards. The Latin words ROTAS OPERA TENET AREPO SATOR can be translated *The Creator guides the wheels with care.*

Although based in Scotland, Gerald Ogilvie Laing is a sculptor of world-wide reputation and exhibits his work in many countries. He has also executed another recent Edinburgh commission, this time to mark the fiftieth anniversary, in 1991, of the Edinburgh Federation of Master Builders, and this work, representing the famous but fictitious character Sherlock Holmes, has been sited near the birthplace (now demolished) of his creator, Sir Arthur Conan Doyle, in Picardy Place.

On the linking walls of the arcading in the entrance hall of Tanfield House two commemorative plaques have been placed. One is inscribed (using the same wording as on the original plaque on the previous building), below a representation of the old Tanfield Hall:

1825
TANFIELD HALL
THE FIRST ASSEMBLY OF THE FREE CHURCH OF
SCOTLAND WAS HELD HERE ON 18 MAY 1843 AND
IN THE SAME HALL THE UNION OF THE SECESSION
AND
RELIEF CHURCHES WAS CONSUMMATED 13 MAY 1847

The other records for posterity the day of the Royal opening of the new building:

THE STANDARD LIFE ASSURANCE COMPANY
TANFIELD
THIS BUILDING WAS OPENED
ON THE FIRST DAY OF JULY 1991
BY HER MAJESTY THE QUEEN

In August 1993 a cairn was placed behind the railings and in front of the 'woolstore' on which an engraved tablet carries the same inscription as the Disruption plaque inside the entrance hall.

On an outside wall facing Brandon Terrace, at a low level and best seen from the end of the new bridge over the Water of Leith from Glenogle Road, a stone-carved tablet depicting the Royal Warrant (the Scottish variant of the Royal Coat of Arms) granted to Morrison & Gibb Ltd. is a reminder of a more recent part of the changing history of Tanfield. It was originally situated above the entrance to the Printers and Bookbinders' premises fronting Howard Place.

Tanfield House has won a number of accolades including the E.A.A. Silver Medal, an R.I.B.A. award and the Du Pont Office of the Year Award.

The 'great river of the Water of Leith' flows on, as oblivious of the ongoing alterations upon its banks as of its own diminished waters which were once so troublesome a barrier to travellers on the road to Trinity and the shores of Forth till the torrent was bridled by a steep stone arch in the mid-eighteenth century. And here, at its Bridge, the northern boundary of Canonmills is reached, while beyond stretch out the lands of Inverleith.

CHAPTER 6

Origins

In the great charter granted by King David I to the Abbey of Holyrood in 1143, wrote John Russell in *The Story of Leith*:

> There is engrossed a long list of the many possessions be-stowed upon it by its royal founder, and among these are the lands of North Leith and that part of South Leith which now extends from the present Coalhill to the Vaults. These lands, along with those of South Leith, then formed part of a wide area round the mouth of the river known as In-verleith, and are designated in the Abbey charter as 'that part of Inverleith which is nearest the harbour'. These words would seem to show that even at this early date Leith had started on its career as a port. The shortened form of the name, Leith, early became specially applied to the town, while the longer form, Inverleith, like the name Inveresk at Musselburgh, was restricted to the lands farther up the river.

The baronial estate of Inverleith (a huge estate the break-up of which started as long ago as the sixteenth century) is of ancient origin also and is mentioned in the charters of Robert the Bruce. In the fifteenth century it came into the possession of a family called Touris, or

Towers, who, like the Napiers of Merchiston, were early instances of merchants becoming landowners and, as John Russell comments, taking a place in the aristocracy without relinquishing trade, as custom would have compelled them to do in France or Germany, and it did not pass out of their hands until 1648. From a charter of 1605 it would appear that the old fortalice of Wardie, or Granton, was owned by Sir John Tours or Touris of Inverleith and James Grant states that the old fortalice of the extinct Touris race 'stood on the highest ground of Inverleith, a little way west of where we find the modern house now embosomed among luxuriant timber', and that of the old castle not a vestige - not even its ancient dovecot - remained in 1880. The archery butts, which are referred to later, were the sole survivors.

John Russell discounts the story of 'the ancient gardener of Trinity Grove' (a house, though no longer known by that name, which is still extant in Trinity Road) making his way 'to Holyrood with his basket of nettle tops over his arm for "sallets" to the queen' as that house was not built till long after Mary Queen of Scots' time. But it is not impossible that he could have been bringing them from gardens on the extensive Touris lands which included the area on which Trinity was later to be laid out. Equally, the long-dead but still visible Queen Mary's tree, also in Trinity Road, if indeed planted, as it is believed to have been, by her, would not have been placed haphazardly on the Wardie Muir but in the grounds of the Touris-owned Wardie Castle. The Touris family were strong supporters of the Queen.

CHAPTER 7

Beyond the Bridge

The Buildings of Scotland: Edinburgh describes Inverleith as a 'wide plain, chequered with parks and playing fields, only 1 km. downhill from the George Street ridge' and the Water of Leith and Canonmills Bridge may be taken as the southern boundary of the district as it is today. It is also the starting point of the extension of Georgian architecture to the north of the New Town. But before that extension is reached Howard Street comprises a short tenemental row of 1895 on the west, while on the east the tenements of Warriston Place, the even shorter section to the immediate north of the bridge, date from around 1818. Then comes the shallow curve and narrow, elegant houses (into the basements of which the Water of Leith has been known to overflow on rare occasions) of Warriston Crescent. Practically complete by 1830, all but those at the extreme western end still have their uninterrupted view across the Warriston playing fields. This Georgian crescent was built on the Warriston House estate and faces Eildon Street across the playing fields.

No. 10 Warriston Crescent has been associated with the name of Chopin ever since he stayed here in 1848. A bronze plaque on the wall gives the following information:

Fryderyk Chopin (1810 - 1849), Polish Composer, stayed here on the occasion of his concert in Edinburgh on the 4th of October, 1848. To commemorate the hundredth anniversary of this event, this plaque was placed by the Polish community and their Scottish friends in 1948.

No. 10 Warriston Crescent where Chopin stayed on his visit to Edinburgh in 1848. A commemorative plaque can be seen on the wall between the two ground-floor windows.

Fryderyk Franciszek Chopin spent the latter years of his life in Paris and it was from that city, although seriously ill with tuberculosis, that he came to Edinburgh where another, now demolished, building at Nos. 68 - 73 Queen Street also perpetuated his memory. On the walls of Erskine House (built in 1964 on the site of the Edinburgh Merchant Company school, The Edinburgh Ladies' College (now the Mary Erskine School) which incorporated the original Hopetoun Rooms of 1827 by Thomas Hamilton) can be read:

1810 - 1849. On the site of this building Fryderyk Chopin gave his final concert in the Hopetoun Rooms, on 4 October 1848.

When the world-famous composer and pianist, who had been born near Warsaw, arrived in the city he was greeted by Dr Adam Lyszczynski who had come to Scotland as a refugee subsequent to the Polish uprising in 1830. He had studied medicine which he later practised from his Warriston Crescent home to which he and his British wife now invited Chopin, and it was here that he lived during his visit to Edinburgh. Returning to Paris, Chopin died there the following year.

Basements in Warriston Crescent were flooded shortly after the Second World War when serious overflowing took place on the Water of Leith. Downstream, the inundation affected the Powderhall Greyhound Racing Stadium at Beaverhall Road as well when a number of dogs had to be taken out by boat. Among those who assisted in the rescue operation was Sir Andrew Murray (1903 - 77), Lord Provost of the city from 1947 to 1951, who at that time resided at No. 20 Warriston Crescent.

Howard Place, immediately north of Warriston Crescent on the main road to Goldenacre (and occupying the east side only of the street so that the house numbers are consecutive), was designed by James Gillespie Graham (1777 - 1855) in 1809, sixteen years before Huntly Street with which it has some affinity in name as already mentioned. This was one of the first Georgian streets to incorporate front gardens, a layout which can be seen in Comely Bank, built shortly after 1817, as well. The most interesting house in Howard Place is also one of the most interesting houses in Edinburgh. This is No. 8 where, as recorded on a plaque beside the door, Robert Louis Stevenson (1850 - 94) was born 'in a comfortable ground-floor bedroom overlooking the back garden', as James Pope Hennessy has described it in his Life of Stevenson. He was not impressed with the street, however, the houses in which he thought, writing in 1974, 'modest, squat and almost mean.' But he was more enthusiastic about their interiors. The outer hall at No. 8 gave, he said, 'an impression of order and even spaciousness.' Through the inner doorway 'may be seen a good, wide staircase, winding up to a large double drawing-room above. The rooms in this house in Howard Place are lofty and dignified. They have about them an air of classical restraint.'

The low-lying position of Howard Place made the house damp and unsuitable for the delicate boy who had inherited from his mother a weakness of the chest. So in 1853 the family removed to No. 1 Inverleith Terrace, a street which runs, on the opposite side of the road, at right angles to Howard Place. But it was no better, the house being on the corner and exposed to the Edinburgh winds in addition to the prevailing dampness, as the outgoing tenants, William Edmondstoune Aytoun, Professor of Rhetoric at Edinburgh University and contributor to *Blackwood's Magazine*, and his wife had discovered. The next move, in 1857 when Louis was six, was therefore to the higher ground, uphill from Inverleith, at No. 17 Heriot Row, a house which became the Edinburgh home of the poet and novelist for the rest of his life. The Inverleith Terrace house was not on the present corner but a little to the west, the corner building which can be seen today being of later date.

No. 8 Howard Place contained for many years a memorial museum to the writer which was open to the public, but the Stevenson relics were removed (when it became once more a private residence) and taken to Lady Stair's House in the Lawnmarket where they are now exhibited along with those of Burns and Scott. Among the letters, manuscripts, portraits and photographs, and many articles which had belonged to 'Cummy' (his nurse Alison Cunningham) in the R.L.S. collection is a linen-press made by the disreputable Deacon Brodie and said to have been used by Stevenson and W.E. Henley.

The poet William Ernest Henley (1849 - 1903) knew Stevenson well and collaborated with him in an unsuccessful attempt to write a play on the subject of Deacon

The birthplace of Robert Louis Stevenson at No. 8 Howard Place.

Brodie who was later used as the prototype for *Dr Jekyll and Mr Hyde* by R.L. Stevenson himself. The Henleys lived 'a few doors from R.S.L.'s birthplace', as Eve Blantyre Simpson, daughter of Sir James Young Simpson, wrote in her book *The R.L. Stevenson Originals*. Their only child, 'a beautiful daughter', was born there but died shortly afterwards in London, her 'brief years' having been spent in Edinburgh in Howard Place. The house was No. 11 and it was during their stay there that Henley was editor of the *Scots Observer*. Here they were visited by the playwright J.M. Barrie who took a particular interest in Margaret, the little daughter, who used to call him 'Friendy-Wendy'. This gave Barrie the name which he was later to immortalise in *Peter Pan*.

In Howard Place also was the residence of Wendy Wood (1892 -1981) who, along with the Scottish Patriots, an organisation which she founded in 1949, had her home at No. 31. Her own Scottish connection consisted of a maternal grandfather who farmed a Highland croft. Although born in England, she spent her early childhood in South Africa and came to Scotland, where she attended boarding-school, at the age of twelve.

In her early twenties she became strongly committed to the cause of Scottish Nationalism, becoming a member of the Home Rule Association at its inauguration in 1916 and a founder member of the Scottish National Party at its commencement in 1928. Much given to single, dramatic acts of defiance against English violations of the 1707 Treaty of Union, she cheerfully went to jail for brief periods on more than one occasion. The incident, however, for which she is principally remembered belongs to her later years when she opposed the Government's refusal, in 1971, to establish a Scottish Convention by a hunger strike. Her 'fast to the death' ended a week later in response to the entreaties of many people, not all of them her active supporters, to abandon such a desperate stand in a battle she could not hope to win.

Wendy Wood had other strings to her bow as well as the nationalism which was undoubtedly her first love. She was also a writer, a sculptor and an artist, having studied painting in London under Sickert in earlier days. Throughout her life she continued to paint and exhibited regularly at the Royal Scottish Academy at The Mound where, at the city's 'Speakers' Corner', her voice was often to be heard setting out with passion her case for Nationalism.

No. 34 Howard Place was the home of Lewis Spence (1874 - 1955), poet, anthropologist and mythologist. At the centenary of his birth in 1974 it was written of him that his 'researches into the style and language of the Makars can be said to have given the cue to the Scottish literary renaissance.' In *The Penguin Book of Scottish Verse* the Scottish poet Tom Scott speaks of Spence's 'recognition of the need to redeem and intellectualize Scots and to revive the great pre-Reformation tradition', which made him in this respect 'something of a forerunner of Hugh MacDiarmid.'

In *The Outlines of Mythology*, written during the Second World War, Lewis Spence set out 'to provide a definite view of the general principles which govern mythic science and to survey the conclusions of modern research concerning its nature as well as to furnish some account of the larger problems associated with it as a whole.' The ancient Greeks, he says, understood the word 'myth' rather differently from its accepted meaning in present-day English. As coined by them, it meant 'the thing spoken' - such as a speech or tale. 'By special application, however, it came to mean a tale concerned with the gods and their deeds or adventures.' He then goes on to deal with the making of myth, the great mythic systems of the world and ends with his conclusions concerning the nature of myth.

As a poet he has been somewhat neglected in the later twentieth century but he wrote some original work in Scots as well as English which deserves to be remembered, such as *The Prows o'Reekie*:

O wad this braw hie-heapit toun
Sail aff like an enchanted ship,
Drift owre the world's seas up and doun,
And kiss wi' Venice lip to lip,
Or anchor into Naples' Bay
A misty island far astray,
Or set her rock to Athens' wa',
Pillar to pillar, stane to stane,
The cruikit spell o' her backbane,
Yon shadow-mile o' spire and vane,
Wad ding them a', wad ding them a'!
Cadiz wad tine the admiralty

O' yonder emerod fair sea,
Gibraltar frown for frown exchange
Wi' Nigel's crags at elbuck-range,
The rose-red banks o' Lisbon make
Mair room in Tagus for her sake.

A hoose is but a puppet-box
To keep life's images frae knocks,
But mannikins scrieve oot their sauls
Upon its craw-steps and its walls;
Whaur hae they writ them mair sublime
Than on yon gable-ends o'time?

and *The Doves of St Giles*:

Around St Paul's the pigeons fly
Like azure shadows from the sky,
And people throw them crumbs of food,
And joy in their blue multitude.

But when I pass St Giles's crown,
And northern psalms, like doves, come down,
I know celestial reasons why
Martyrs for such bright birds could die.

There is a keen, high rapture there,
Stark, and most excellently bare,
A lustre of the naked walls
Such as I never saw in Paul's.

In the first volume of her Autobiography, *Curriculum Vitae*, Muriel Spark tells of winning first prize in a poetry competition in 1932. One of the good effects of this event, she says, was her meeting with 'the adjudicator of the prize, Lewis Spence, an Edinburgh poet and considerable man of letters.' Accompanied by one of her teachers, she 'went to tea with him at his home' where they talked about poetry. During the course of the conversation he told her 'Of course you will write as a profession', a prophecy which has been amply fulfilled.

Inverleith Terrace faces the southern side of the Royal Botanic Garden, the houses overlooking the Water of Leith at the back, and here stands the former First Church of Christ Scientist, an interesting building designed by the architect Ramsay R. Traquair (c.1874 - 1952). He was the son of Phoebe Traquair (1852 - 1936) (the painter who executed the now water-damaged murals in the former Catholic Apostolic Church at the corner of Mansfield Place and East London Street to which reference has already been made) and a pupil of Sir Robert Lorimer. The church was based on old St Giles in Elgin (*The Buildings of Scotland: Edinburgh*) and its saddleback tower is something of a landmark in the area. The tunnel-vaulted interior was 'flooded with light' from the large windows. This interior was in recent years reconstructed to accommodate an education centre for the adjoining St Colm's College (No. 23 Inverleith Terrace) 'designed as the United Free Church Training Institute for Lady Missionaries by Gordon L. Wright' (*The Buildings of Scotland: Edinburgh*) in 1908. The College chapel contains a stained-glass window depicting Christ the Light of the World by William Hole (1846 - 1917) of whose mural paintings in the former St James' Church at Goldenacre (and residence in Inverleith) an account is given later.

St Colm's College itself has also been renovated, an appeal for £300,000 having been made to meet the whole costs involved. The College and the Centre, which is known as the Annie Small Centre after the first principal of the Women's Missionary Training Institute, as it was called when it was moved from Atholl Crescent to

Inverleith, were opened and dedicated by Professor James Whyte in 1989.

St Colm's has an interesting link with the preservation of Moubray House, one of the oldest buildings in the High Street of Edinburgh, at a time prior to the introduction of the statutory safeguards which apply today. The Cockburn Association, having obtained possession of the house shortly before the First World War and requiring from financial necessity to let the premises, were anxious to avoid any damage to the interior while it was in process of gradual restoration. In *Scotia's Darling Seat*, written and published for the Association in 1926, the Edinburgh historian Rosaline Masson wrote, 'After the War . . . the house was let on a ninety-nine years' lease, with necessary provisions in the agreement assuring against any alteration of the antique features.' The upper portion of the house was 'occupied by the Women's Missionary College of the U.F. Church, Inverleith Terrace, to which body four years later, the whole lease was ascribed. So was Moubray House saved'.

CHAPTER 8

Warriston

Howard Place terminates at Eildon Street which runs at right angles to Inverleith Row on the north side of Warriston Playing Fields, originally known as the School Board Recreation Park. These playing fields were laid out, as were Warriston Crescent and Eildon Street, on Heriot Trust land which was once part of the West Warriston estate when the site of the present tennis courts was an ornamental pond, the cause of a continuing tendency to waterlogging after heavy rain. In the 1890s the southern section with the tennis courts and a bowling green was known as Warriston Park, and the northern section in front of Eildon Street was the Edinburgh Institution (later Melville College and now Stewarts Melville) Cricket Ground. Eildon Street, a terrace of bay-windowed Victorian and then, beyond No. 18, Edwardian houses, faces Warriston Crescent across the playing fields and was deliberately sited to take advantage of the view southwards to the skyline of the Old Town.

Beyond Eildon Street is the entrance drive (now Eildon Terrace) to the former (West) Warriston House (its one remaining gate-pier disappeared a few years ago), the site of which was left unbuilt on for some considerable time after the first modern houses were introduced. A two-storey Georgian villa, the successor to an earlier residence built by the Somervilles, and entered by a double stair across a half-sunk basement, with balustrading at roof level and two single-storey side pavilions, Warriston House was built in 1784 and demolished in 1966. The builder was William Ramsay, the Edinburgh banker, of Ramsay, Bonar & Company, one of the banks whose loans enabled the construction of the New Town to be

This solitary gate-pier stood for many years at the entrance to the demolished (West) Warriston House long after modern houses had been built beside the driveway.

financed. His partner was Andrew Bonar of East Warriston House.

In *Traditions of Edinburgh* Robert Chambers mentions him in connection with a club which met in Canonmills. 'About 1790', he writes, 'a club of first-rate citizens used to meet each Saturday afternoon for a country dinner, in a tavern . . . in the village of Canonmills. . . . Originally the fraternity were contented with a very humble room; but in time they got an addition built to the house for their accommodation, comprehending one good-sized room with two windows, in one of which is a pane containing an olive-dove; in the other, one containing a wheat-sheaf, both engraved with a diamond.' The engraving had been executed by 'William Ramsay then residing at Warriston.' Here, we are told, 'he took great delight to drink claret on the Saturdays, though he had such a

View from Gosford Place of the demolition of Chancelot Flour Mills in 1972. (Photograph courtesy Mrs Joan Milne).

paradise near at hand to retire to . . .' By 1847 one of the window panes had been destroyed and both tavern and windows have long since been swept away.

In the early sixteenth century the old estate of Warriston had been in the possession of the Somerville family who built the original house on the site of the later mansion. In 1579 'the house or fortalice of Warriston' was beseiged by, among others, the Rocheids, who were later to play so prominent a part in the annals of Inverleith, at which time it was the dwelling-place of William Somerville. For this 'outrage' they appear to have been acquitted. The Somervilles were succeeded in the 1580s by the family of Kincaid.

A tragedy which has been recorded as having taken place in the earlier house has been found, as a result of recent research, more probably to have occurred in East

Warriston House (which is mentioned later). The story is to the effect that Jean Livingston, the wife of John Kincaid of Warriston, being badly treated by her husband, took the misguided step of employing a hired assassin, in the person of Robert Weir, a servant of her father, to do away with him. Both were tried and sentenced to death. The Lady of Warriston, said Charles Kirkpatrick Sharpe, who wrote an account of these events, displayed a spirit of great contrition before being executed by the 'Maiden' at the Girth Cross of Edinburgh, prior to which she read an address to the assembled spectators who were moved to compassion by her serenity and courage. She was only twenty-one years of age.

In his book *Sciennes and The Grange* Malcolm Cant tells how, after the destruction at the Reformation of the Convent, founded in 1518, of St Catherine of Sienna and the dispersal of the convent community in 1567, the last prioress 'feued the lands to Henry Kincaid, second son of John Kincaid of Warriston. It is uncertain how long the lands were in the possession of the Kincaids, but by the middle of the seventeenth century' they had passed to other hands.

Sir Archibald Johnston of Warriston (1611 - 63), a Lord of Session in 1641 who was granted a peerage by Oliver Cromwell, was a subsequent owner. The honour cost him his life, however, as he was executed by Charles II after the Restoration. He had taken the title of Lord Warriston. Johnston of Warriston, wrote Gordon Donaldson in *The Faith of the Scots*, became 'leader of the extreme wing of the Covenanting Party' and he is said to have had a hand in drafting the National Covenant itself in 1638.

The last owner of (West) Warriston House was John Best for whose business of John Best (Edinburgh) Ltd., public works contractors, he opened an office within the house. In July 1930 a garden fête was held here by Mr and Mrs Best at which a speech was made by Ramsay MacDonald during his second term of office as Prime Minister. In the course of the Second World War the ornamental wrought-iron gates were put into store to avoid their being taken, as a result of Government instructions, to be used as grist to the mill of wartime munitions manufacture. Many front gardens lost their railings for this intended purpose, though how much was actually made use of was a matter of speculation at the time. After the war these beautiful gates were placed within Drummond Place Gardens where they can still be seen inside the western entrance gate.

'When the feuing at Warriston', wrote Rosaline Masson, 'threatened the beautiful old trees surrounding Warriston House (the trees that little Louis Stevenson, in his childhood walks with "Cummie", used to gaze at through the openwork of the wrought-iron gates of Warriston House) the Cockburn Council met to consider what could be done to save them. The plans of the builders, submitted to them, showed a dense line of tall houses and a narrow street. They then asked for a calculation of the money loss if the buildings were thrown back to a farther distance from Inverleith Row, so that the front line of trees could be preserved, and laid information before the proprietors of the neighbourhood. The proprietors met to consider it, Mr Mitchell, the Secretary of the Cockburn Association, being present. The offer of the builders (£3,000 immediate payment, and £3,000 later) was too costly to be met by the feuars; but the feuing was restricted owing to Warriston House being let with some of its grounds. This saved at any rate the trees near the house - that magnificent group of ancient sentinel trees, high against the sky. The recommendations of the Cockburn prevailed, for there are those trees to-day, the last of the trees of Warriston; and when the wrought-iron gates open and disclose them, they take the breath away by their dignity and beauty.' And, although the gates and many of the 'sentinel trees' have gone, some of the latter are there yet behind the wall over which their branches in due season spread out their still abundant leaves above the pavement.

'The estate of Warriston (formerly West Warriston)', says *The Buildings of Scotland: Edinburgh*, 'lay on the east side of the road from Canonmills to Trinity', and East Warriston lay beyond it to the east. East Warriston House was entered from the northern section of Warriston Road and was built, according to most authorities, in 1818 (although recent research places it slightly earlier) by the banker, Andrew Bonar, already mentioned. The architect has not so far been traced. This two-storey villa was converted to the Warriston Crematorium by Sir Robert Lorimer's architectural practice, Lorimer & Matthew, in 1929 (the most original part remaining being the north side) when it passed out of the hands of the Bonar family. In the 1930s the registered office of 'Edinburgh Crematorium Limited, Crematorium, Warriston Road' was Heriot Hill House, No. 1 Broughton Road in upper Canonmills, to which reference has already been made.

Eastwards of East Warriston House, between the Water of Leith and Dalmeny Road, lay the Chancelot Flour Mills (not demolished till 1972) which were relocated in 1954 at the Western Harbour at Leith Docks, where they are still extant, under the name of Chancelot Mill Ltd. It has been claimed that the original Chancelot Mills area was offered for sale, many years ago, as a 'chance lot' and that the name lingered and became perpetuated. It has been used for several streets in the vicinity. Agnew Terrace, off Ferry Road, takes its name from Lieut. Col. G. Agnew, a former resident in East Warriston House.

Around East Warriston House other 'quaint little mansionhouses', all now vanished, were Redbraes, idyllic of situation within a loop of the Water of Leith, Powderhall beside and called after the gunpowder manufactory, and Beaverhall which superseded the earlier skin works where the popular beaver hats were produced from imported hides for over a hundred years. Transatlantic shipping brought the beaver skins to the port of Leith and in return, under a curious system of barter, 'notorious vagabonds' were herded from the prisons to the holds of creaking, over-crowded vessels, their eventual fate, to be sold as slaves in the American plantations or the West Indies, being, if they survived the voyage, sometimes a worse alternative to incarceration in inhuman jails. The Rev. D.P. Thomson, writing in *By the Water of Leith* (a history of McDonald Road Church, demolished in 1977, and its parish) notes that among such 'vagabonds' were included many who had only committed petty offences and even, for their steadfast adherence to their principles, 'poor Covenanters'. It is only fair to acknowledge, he adds, 'that once on the other side of the water many of the victims were kindly treated, becoming in time the owners of small plantations of their own.'

In the eighteenth century that part of the lands of Powderhall on which the disused hat factory still stood was purchased and the house called Beaverhall was built beside it. Beaverhall Road and Beaverbank Place were later laid out across the site, near the Water of Leith, when both the former factory and the house had been demolished.

Around 1870 the Powderhall estate was bought for the purposes of laying out a sports ground, and in 1883 the Scottish Amateur Athletic Championships were first held at Old Powderhall. But it was at the new Beaverhall Road Stadium that Eric Liddell 'repeated in 1922', as D.P. Thomson has written, 'his "Double" of the previous year in the sprints, on the track on which he had got his training.' The athletic centre was converted to use as a racing track for the Greyhound Racing Association in 1926. Powderhall Stadium changed hands in 1990 when it was purchased for over three million pounds and a planned leisure complex introduced to augment greyhound racing which still takes pride of place on three nights a week. The possibility of the sale of this eleven-acre site at Beaverhall has again arisen in 1993.

Redbraes House, on land 'commonly called the Reidbraes', was well known for its ornamental pond, later used for public skating during the winter months, which was created out of a natural bog.

James Balfour, whose son James became the first Balfour of Pilrig and from whose family R.L. Stevenson was descended, was one of the partners who owned the powder-mill at Powderhall. The Edinburgh Cleansing Department's Powderhall Refuse Depot was built in Broughton Road in 1893 when the refuse carts were horse-drawn, the stables afterwards being put to good use for many years as the Corporation's Dog and Cat Home, later moved to Seafield. The furnaces, however, were in use until 1984 when, in response to repeated complaints, the tall chimney, which had spread its polluting soot over a wide surrounding area, was taken down. Logie Green House stood on the site of the west side of Logie Green Road and mill-wheels were turned by the main, or 'great', lade at Logie Green as well. St Philip's Scottish Episcopal Church, on the corner of Broughton Road and Logie Green Road, has from its inception had a close connection with the former St James' Church at the north end of Inverleith Row and, for that reason, is incorporated in the history of the latter church at Goldenacre.

Immediately opposite the Crematorium is one of the entrances to Warriston Cemetery which can also be approached from Inverleith Row via Warriston Gardens, a street which forms the southern boundary of George Heriot's Sports Ground access to which is also obtained from Inverleith Row. The cemetery lies between the Water of Leith at Warriston Road and the east end of Warriston Gardens.

The printer and horticulturist (and successor to James Eyre in Canonmills House) Patrick Neill was also con-

A view of Edinburgh from Warriston Cemetery showing the three-arched Canonmills Bridge a few years after its construction and the steeples of St Mary's and St Stephen's Churches to the east and west. (From *Old and New Edinburgh* by James Grant)

cerned in the planning of Edinburgh's new cemeteries
which were laid out during the 1840s. Decisions as to
appropriate sites were taxing civic minds and Dr Neill
submitted that The Meadows or the King's Park (a large
area near the foot of Arthur's Seat) should be considered,
the former being ruled out, however, as building on The
Meadows was prohibited by the Improvement Act of
1827. Someone else had quite seriously proposed the sum-
mit of Arthur's Seat! In the event Neill's plans came to
nothing and on the establishment of The Edinburgh Cemetery Company in 1842 fourteen acres of land were
acquired by them on the northern side of the Water of
Leith at Warriston and the New Edinburgh Cemetery, as
it was called at first, was opened the following year.

George Mackay Brown has written of a discussion in
the *Orcadian* newspaper about the merits or demerits of
the designations "kirkyard", "cemetery" or "graveyard".
The preference turned out to be for "kirkyard" 'because
it undoubtedly is the most euphonious of the three'. But
around the middle of the nineteenth century it was the
"garden cemetery", landscaped and planted with trees,
that was all the rage and Warriston was the first of its
kind in Edinburgh. It was designed by David Cousin, an
architect who was also responsible for several others
which were soon to follow, and has been described (in
Edinburgh: An Illustrated Architectural Guide, 1992) as
a new 'fever cemetery begun as a result of the cholera
epidemic and modelled on the cemetery of Père Lachaise
in Paris'. The victims of cholera and other diseases represented a health hazard if buried in shallow graves,
especially if the graveyards were within densely populated
areas.

Warriston Cemetery, 'with a gentle slope to the sun
and commanding a magnificent view of the city', was,
says Grant, 'laid out with very considerable taste.' It
could be approached from Warriston Gardens or, by way
of Warriston Road at Canonmills, 'from a narrow lane

leading to East Warriston House.' At the Warriston Gardens entrance is a lodge which was not built until 1931 and which has in recent years been used as a children's playschool.

Some architectural skill was exercised in the range of catacombs or vaults built in a Tudor-revival style and consisting of a 'corridor for mural monuments, top-lit by gratings in the terrace above' (*The Buildings of Scotland: Edinburgh*) also designed by Cousin which was doubled in length in 1862. Interments were made either in the ground below or above ground in lead coffins. The balustraded terrace was built above the buttressed frontage of the range, as well as a little mortuary chapel with stained glass windows for Episcopalian use which has now disappeared. These catacombs are the largest and finest in any of the nineteenth century Edinburgh cemeteries.

The architect J. Dick Peddie (1824 - 91), who was responsible for the extension of the catacombs, also designed, in 1845 and in the same Tudor-revival style, the tunnel with its ornamental arches which links the north and south sections of the cemetery beneath the old Edinburgh and North Leith railway embankment. The north section was laid out in 1905.

Of the many sepulchral monuments in the cemetery the most interesting and unusual was the mortuary chapel above the grave of Mrs Mary Ann Robertson (1826 - 58), the daughter of Brigadier-General Manson of the Bombay Artillery (*The Edinburgh Graveyard Guide* by Michael T.R.B. Turnbull) who died at the early age of 32. In white marble of Gothic design by the London sculptor H.S. Liefchild, this shrine was surely as touching an expression of grief as could be found in any place of burial. It was given a ruby-tinted glazed roof so that anyone looking into it would see the carved recumbent figure on the tomb below through rose-coloured glass. As a consequence this monument acquired the name of 'the Red

Lady' and was much frequented by those who took a Sunday afternoon walk through the cemetery. The garden cemeteries, owned by joint-stock companies and run for profit but looked after well, were places of regular week-end resort in Victorian days. Unfortunately the Red Lady's tomb has been vandalised in recent times like so many others in the city's cemeteries which have been in less frequent use since the introduction of cremation. The ruby glass has gone and little remains of the entire memorial but some of the stone foundations embedded in the Warriston earth.

On the slope of the terrace, along with some other members of his family, lie the mortal remains of that great medical doctor, philanthropist and 'Renaissance man' Sir James Young Simpson (1811 - 70) who, at his house at 52 Queen Street, discovered the anaesthetic effects of chloroform upon himself and his assistants. This had been supplied to him by Duncan, Flockhart and Company, the well-known Edinburgh chemists, who at that time had a physic garden in Warriston. Born in Bathgate, where his father was the village baker, and of Huguenot ancestry through his mother whose maiden name was Jervais, he took the title Sir James Young Simpson of Strathavon on receiving a baronetcy in 1866. In 1843 he had been among those who marched down to Tanfield for the inauguration of the Free Church of Scotland and appears in the subsequent Disruption painting by D.O. Hill.

Worn out by a life dedicated to the welfare of others, and in particular to the poor, Simpson died at his Queen Street home at the age of 58. His family declined the proposal that he should be buried in Westminster Abbey, where a portrait medallion was placed instead in his memory, and he was laid to rest beside those of his children who had predeceased him, the crowds lining the streets which led to Warriston witnessing the poignant sight of his empty carriage following the hearse. Eve

Blantyre Simpson, his youngest daughter, wrote the life of her father in the *Famous Scots* series in 1896 and was buried beside him in January 1920.

Here too lies the outstanding Scottish landscape painter Horatio MacCulloch (1805 - 67), the son of a Glasgow weaver. Born in that city in the year of Trafalgar and given the Christian name of Admiral Nelson, the hero of the hour, he later came to Edinburgh where he stayed at No. 12 Howard Place before removing to Danube Street in Stockbridge and, at the end of his life, to Trinity. His monument, designed by James Drummond, R.S.A., is in the form of a Celtic cross decorated with a palette and brushes and a laurel wreath on one side of the base and, on the other, with a bas-relief of his favourite dogs.

The name of the poet and essayist Alexander Smith (1829 - 69) (a near neighbour in Trinity of Horatio MacCulloch to whom his wife Flora was related) is not as well known today as it once was. Born in Kilmarkock, he was the son of a lace pattern designer who moved to Paisley when Alexander was still a child and, fairly soon afterwards, to Glasgow where his son took up the same occupation as his father. After submitting, in 1851, some verses to the Dundee poet The Rev. George Gilfillan, who praised his work and used his influence on Smith's behalf, publication in literary journals followed, and long poems such as his first, *A Life Drama*, were well received, ten thousand copies of that work being sold in Great Britain and 'the Colonies' as well as an American edition. Wishing to free himself from his pattern making, he sought more satisfying and congenial employment, and this materialised in 1854 when he was appointed Secretary to the University of Edinburgh at a salary of £150 per annum. This was increased some years later when he took on the additional duties of Registrar and Secretary to the University Council.

Now launched as a poet, in 1857 he married Flora Macdonald of Skye who was, says his biographer John

Alexander Smith, poet and essayist, was buried in Warriston Cemetery beside other famous names in Edinburgh history.

Hogben, 'a blood relation of the Flora Macdonald of unfading romance and fame', and they eventually settled at No. 12 Boswall Road in a Georgian house which at that time was called Gesto Villa. Here, from the rear windows, he could look out at the dramatic skyline of the Old Town which was the inspiration of his poem *A Vision of Edinburgh as seen from Trinity*, the title being abbreviated to *Edinburgh* in some anthologies. This was later published in his *City Poems* together with his corresponding work *Glasgow*.

In 1863 *Dreamthorp: a Book of Essays written in the Country* was brought out which had 'certainly more readers than any of his other books' as Hogben wrote, adding that 'it is not too much to say that there are passages in it that may deliberately challenge comparison with the work of any English essayist.' The little town of Dreamthorp was based on Linlithgow, its palace becoming a castle and its loch a lake to give it more appeal, it may be supposed, to English readers. He contributed to Blackwood's and many other magazines, 'did a considerable amount of work for the *Encyclopaedia Britannica, Chambers Encyclopaedia* and Mackenzie's *Biographical Dictionary*, and wrote on Skye as well where he 'had passed many summers'. Trevor Royle has described his *A Summer in Skye* as 'an early travel book' containing 'a stunning description of Edinburgh in winter.' But overwork reduced his resistance to illness and he succumbed to the 'typhoid fever complicated with diphtheria' which caused his untimely death.

Many tributes were paid to him including the heartfelt lines by Sheriff Nicolson, '. . . Unlike many whose whole goodness and fine sentiment is put into their books, his life and character were as beautiful as anything he wrote.' John Hogben described Warriston Cemetery and Smith's burial there in memorable words:

There is no more beautiful cemetery in Edinburgh than Warriston. The Dean may have a more dignified solemnity, with its sentinel yews, but Warriston heaves the green but marbled shoulders of God's Acre to the sun and to the south. From its heights the views of Edinburgh are wonderfully fine, and it is musical with birds that help to keep the thoughts above the daisy-starred grass that grows and withers over the silent dead. It was here . . . that the body of Alexander Smith was laid. The burial-place is in the extreme north-east corner of the cemetery, and it is marked by a finely decorated Iona Cross, bearing the words "Alexander Smith, Poet and Essayist". The Cross was designed by his friend James Drummond, R.S.A., but Sir J. Noel Paton, R.S.A., had also some share in the decoration. The bronze medallion likeness was the work of a third friend - William Brodie, R.S.A.

His grave is on the east side of the terrace. One of his children about whom he had written lovingly, a daughter called Flora after her mother, only survived him by two months.

The Scottish painter Robert Scott Lauder (1803 - 69) is also buried here, commemorated by a Sicilian marble slab with a portrait medallion by the sculptor John Hutchison. He and his brother were natives of Silvermills and some particulars of their lives have already been given.

The famous Edinburgh publisher, born in the city at the time of the Enlightenment and whose statue is in East Princes Street Gardens, Adam Black (1784 - 1874), was also interred in Warriston Cemetery. He gained experience in bookselling in London before returning, in 1807, to Edinburgh where his premises in South Bridge became well known to authors and their reading public. 'The cradle of his fortunes', as Grant puts it, 'was that little shop which till 1821 was deemed ample enough for the . . . requirements of all Scotland.' His house was at No. 38 Drummond Place. Twice Lord Provost of Edinburgh, he was also returned to the House of Commons as member for the city, in succession to Lord Macaulay, when 'beyond his seventieth year.'

Adam Black purchased the copyright of the Waverley Novels and other works by Sir Walter Scott and also took over publication of *The Edinburgh Review* after the collapse of Constable & Co. in 1826.

The firm of James Ballantine & Son, and other firms incorporating the Ballantine name, were prolific artists in stained glass from a family which spanned at least two generations during the nineteenth and twentieth centuries. The earliest was James Ballantine (1808 - 77), who was also a poet and an author, and his grave is to be found in Warriston Cemetery. His literary works include *The Gaberlunzie's Wallet*, his best known publication, valuable prose descriptions of the Edinburgh of his time, treatises and other writings on stained-glass and a Life of the Stockbridge-born artist David Roberts.

James Ballantine's major professional work was carried out as a consequence of his employment by The Royal Commission on the Fine Arts to execute the stained-glass windows in the House of Lords in London, but his expertise was sought by the architects of many churches and other buildings in Edinburgh. 'The ever reliable but never brilliant Ballantines', bluntly states *The Buildings of Scotland: Edinburgh*, purveyed stained-glass to churches of all denominations from St Giles, St Cuthbert's and St John's to Morningside, Pilrig and Newhaven. 'Old' Greyfriars, the first parish church to be built in Edinburgh after the Reformation, was first also in the installation of stained-glass, the five Lancets of the east window here being by Ballantine and Allan in 1857. The west window, depicting the Resurrection, dates from 1898 and was the work of A. Ballantine and Gardiner. Their last Edinburgh commission was for the Reid Memorial Church around 1930. When signing their windows they were in the habit of spelling their name Ballantyne.

Working from drawings by David Roberts and James Drummond, James Ballantine provided glass for one of the chambers above the statue in the Scott Monument, and the glass depicting the Signs of the Zodiac in the lantern over the oval hall in the Edinburgh Academy is also by him. His glass in the original chapel (now the school hall) at Donaldson's Hospital was blown out by a bomb dropped by a Zeppelin in 1916. This was 'weakly replaced', although a fragment of the original glass is still preserved within the building. He died at his home at Warrender Lodge in Meadow Place aged 69.

Other names, famous in their day, inscribed on the tombstones of Warriston Cemetery include Duncan M'Neil, Lord Colonsay (1794 - 1874), Sir James P. Marwick who was Town Clerk of Glasgow from 1860 till 1873 and Town Clerk of Edinburgh from 1873 to

1903 (the author of many civic books, he died in 1908) and, in the southern section, Robert Young, the Stevenson family's gardener at Swanston. 'Dr Syntax', who is also buried here, was well known in the city in the first half of the nineteenth century. His name was John Sheriff and he was celebrated for his pen-and-ink sketches of note-worthy citizens, particularly among the clergy, of the capital. He often worked during Sunday services and T.M. Tod, in an unusual little book called *Random Notes and Recollections of Edinburgh* published in 1944, says of him that 'on one occasion the minister of St George's had to have him forcibly ejected from the church, as he found it quite impossible to conduct the service with the grotesque figure opposite him deftly plying his pencil.' Engraved on his tombstone are the words *In memory of John Sheriff, who died 17 August 1844, aged 69. Erected by those who mourn the loss of Syntax.*

Two monuments below the terrace commemorate members of the Flockhart family of Messrs. Duncan and Flockhart, and Miss Jane E. Flockhart, the last representative of her line (the old-established Edinburgh chemists), was buried in the cemetery in November 1930.

The Scottish advocate and historian Cosmo Innes, whose last Edinburgh home was Inverleith House, also lies in a Warriston grave. An outline of his life is given under The Royal Botanic Garden.

T.M. Tod recalls 'a stone in Warriston which only bears the words: "A Contrite Sinner". It is said that an Irish clergyman fell into bad company. He lived in Edinburgh under an assumed name for twenty-five years, and left instructions that the above words were to be put above his grave.'

And he also tells the story of a 'terrible adventure in Warriston' Cemetery which befell the unnamed writer of a book called *Edinburgh Dissected*. 'On a winter afternoon', he quotes, 'he entered the Chapel (now removed) and meditated for some time. On coming out he found that a dense fog had enveloped the cemetery. Vividly he describes how he got entangled among tombstones of all sorts and sizes, and his legs were caught by chains separating the graves. After many attempts to find the path to the lodge, he had to spend the night there. The writer tersely says: "I began to feel in all its naked reality the awfulness of my situation." One wonders whether any other person had such a grim experience.'

The future of Edinburgh's cemeteries was the cause of considerable foreboding throughout 1992 after six sites at Saughton, Corstorphine Hill, Merchiston, Newington, Comely Bank and Warriston had been sold in a secret deal to new private owners in spite of several attempts by Edinburgh District Council, who had been outbid by the unknown rival, to purchase them. All had fallen into serious dereliction and complaints were being received from the families of those who had been buried there. They had been in the possession of Crownground, a company which became bankrupt in January of that year, and the sale had been arranged by their liquidators who declined to reveal the name of the purchaser. Fears were immediately expressed that the eighty acres of burial ground would be exploited for financial gain without regard to the wishes of the deceaseds' surviving relatives and descendants. The Commonwealth War Graves Commission also made clear to the Council its concern about the condition of several hundred war graves within these cemeteries. The main reason for the alarm was the possibility that the graveyards would be developed for building purposes, but for this to happen permission would first have to be obtained from both the local authority and the families of the people interred.

The identification of the new owners was disclosed in April. The cemeteries had been acquired by a company called Freshbright Ltd. who were also revealed to be in the property development business and who were opposing the Council's aim of obtaining compulsory purchase orders for the cemeteries at Saughton and Corstorphine Hill.

In the meantime The Scottish Council's Charter for Wildlife was signed in Edinburgh in May 1992 after thirty-one sites, including Holyrood Park, the Braid and Corstorphine Hills, the abandoned city railway lines, the Water of Leith and Warriston Cemetery, had been pinpointed for conservation. Steps were also being taken to place protection orders on two thousand trees at Warriston, Newington and other cemeteries. Only Comely Bank was already covered by a Tree Preservation Order.

So strong was the language of public and official outrage that Freshbright issued a statement to the effect that the cemeteries would be used only as places of burial and commenced a programme of clearing and improving the sites. They were in any case given notice to remove the forests of giant hogweed at Newington and Warriston where it had become a threat to public health. A vigorous campaign was then launched to locate and list the war graves and to have these places of burial brought into public ownership, the outcome being that Newington and Warriston Cemeteries were listed as Grade B sites by Historic Scotland. But a new problem now emerged with the announcement that the cost of burial at the six locations was to be drastically increased, the price being raised from £165 to over £1,000. Permission for a headstone was now £212 in place of the previous £30. This would mean that interment in the original "garden cemeteries" would now be beyond many people's means.

By June 1993 the District Council had approved compulsory purchase orders for Saughton and Corstorphine Hill cemeteries although, concerning them, a public enquiry was still to be held, and had decided to serve orders for compulsory acquisition on the burial grounds at Newington, North Merchiston, Comely Bank and Warriston.

CHAPTER 9

The Royal Botanic Garden

On the west side of Inverleith Row, between Arboretum House (an hotel at the commencement of the Second World War) and the Playfair house at No. 8, is the narrow east gate entrance to The Royal Botanic Garden which, exultingly declares *The Buildings of Scotland: Edinburgh*, includes 'a surprising quantity of architecture' and which extends at the present time across 25 hectares (72 acres). But the Garden pre-dates much of the architecture and has a history which goes back to the seventeenth century at other locations: back, in fact, to the year 1670 when two doctors of medicine began the cultivation of medicinal plants at St Anne's Yard beside Holyrood Abbey on a piece of land just forty feet square which was given the name of The Royal Abbey Garden. It is the second oldest Botanic Garden in Britain, Edinburgh having been preceded by Oxford which founded its Garden in 1632. Many of the plants in the original Botanic Garden were provided by Patrick Murray of Livingston. A separate physic garden also existed on former marshland beside Trinity Hospital, a site now occupied by the platforms and railtracks of the Waverley Station. This Garden is commemorated by a plaque on the outside south wall of the present Booking Hall. Under the heading *The Edinburgh Physic Garden* the plaque is inscribed:

Near this spot from 1675 to 1763 was the Edinburgh Physic Garden, originally founded at Holyrood in 1670 by Sir Robert Sibbald and Sir Andrew Balfour, two of the founders of The Royal College of Physicians of Edinburgh. The garden, under the control of James Sutherland, the first Regius Professor of Botany in the University, was the direct predecessor of the present Royal Botanic Garden. This plaque was erected in 1978 by The Royal College of Physicians of Edinburgh and the Royal Botanic Garden.

Sir Robert Sibbald was the first Professor of Medicine at Edinburgh University and Sir Andrew Balfour, a physician and botanist, is credited with having introduced the manufacture of paper into Scotland.

Part of the Nor' Loch ran through the Trinity Hospital site and when, in 1689, the loch was temporarily drained, the garden was inundated by its polluted waters. When they abated the mud to which the ground had been reduced revealed, to the dismay of its custodians, its impregnation with the contents of the city's drains. Most of the costly collection of rare and delicate plants had been destroyed.

The site of the Trinity Hospital physic garden (which was under the superintendence of James Sutherland, a gardener turned botanist, who in 1683 published his *Hortus Medicus Edinburgensis*, a catalogue of the plants in the Physic Garden, dedicated to the Lord Provost, Sir George Drummond) became more and more unsuited to botanical research but it was not till 1763 that it was relocated on a five-acre area of land at the top of Leith Walk.

In 1761 Dr John Hope (1725 - 86), grandson of Archibald Hope of Rankeillor and great-great-grandson of Sir Thomas Hope of Craighall (the latter having been appointed King's Advocate by Charles I), was chosen to succeed the previous holder of the office of King's Botanist for Scotland and Superintendent of the Royal Botanic Garden in Edinburgh. He was also appointed joint Professor of Botany and Materia Medica in the Faculty of Medicine in the University, having become a member of the Royal College of Physicians of Edinburgh in 1750.

He now set himself to the task of creating a new botanic garden which would unite the collections from the former Royal Abbey location and the subsequent Trinity Hospital Garden on 'a single larger site', as A.G. Morton, FRSE, has written in *John Hope, Scottish Botanist*, 'outside the city, and he cleverly chose a plot of poor but varied soil to the north of Leith Walk, which would not cost a high rent and would be accessible and free of pollution', the original two being 'badly affected by the city smoke'. Sufficient funds were made available to provide hothouses for the more delicate plants and Dr Hope in due course created a pond for aquatic plants and built a substantial, two-storey house for John Williamson, his gardener. This house, now serving as office accommodation, still survives in Haddington Place long after the garden itself had, in James Grant's words, degenerated into 'a species of desolate waste ground, enclosed by a rusty iron railing, with here and there an old tree dying of neglect and decay, till at length innovations swept it away.'

John Hope introduced into Scotland the Linnaean system of plant classification and, at his own expense, commissioned the leading Scottish architect Robert Adam to design a monument to the great Swedish naturalist after his death in 1778. This monument, a square stone pedestal supporting an ornamental urn, and inscribed below a small portrait head

LINNAEO
POSUIT
I HOPE
1779

was re-erected in the Royal Botanic Garden at Inverleith and here it can be seen today on the north side of the glasshouses.

The Leith Walk Garden too became overtaken by urban development and by the second decade of the nineteenth century could no longer be regarded as being 'outside the city'. So it was decided to move again and in 1820 fourteen acres of the Inverleith estate were acquired, later to be extended by additional purchases of adjacent ground.

The lands of Inverleith had passed in 1678, after the time of the Touris ownership, into the hands of Sir James Rocheid who was said to owe his name to a physical peculiarity of a predecessor. This name has for long been in use for the Rocheid Path beside the Water of Leith leading towards Inverleith Park, and was recently adopted for Rocheid Park, a new residential development at East Fettes Avenue. Sir James, while holding the office of Town Clerk, had been suspected of embezzlement, but

The sylvan Rocheid Path by the Water of Leith recalls the Rocheid family, owners of the land and builders of Inverleith House.

appears to have avoided conviction for this and other possible offences. Much more is known about the last member of this family, another James, who, in 1774, built the present Inverleith House in which he lived with his mother, the celebrated Mrs Rocheid of Inverleith, the older house nearby, which had deteriorated to the point of uninhabitability, having had to be vacated.

Lord Cockburn in *Memorials of His Time* gives an eye-witness account of the occupants of Inverleith House. James Rocheid farmed the extensive lands and his mother was a leading light in the famous Edinburgh 'Assemblies' of the day. Having previously been situated in the Old Town, 'in 1785 the "George Square Assembly Rooms" were opened in the lower portion of the tenement in Buccleuch Place facing up George Square. Here "Lady Don and Mrs Rocheid of Inverleith both shone, first as hooped beauties in the minuet and then as ladies of ceremonies." ' These decorously formal functions were finally transferred to the present Assembly Rooms in George Street in 1787.

Lady Don, a 'venerable faded beauty', was about the last person in Edinburgh who kept a private sedan chair. 'Hers stood in the lobby, and was as handsome and comfortable as silk, velvet, and gilding could make it. And, when she wished to use it, two well-known respectable chairmen, enveloped in her livery cloaks, were the envy of their brethren. She and Mrs Rocheid both sat in the Tron Church; and well' did Lord Cockburn remember how he used 'to form one of the group to see these beautiful relics emerge from the coach and the chair.'

Nobody, continues Cockburn, with the exception of the actress Mrs Siddons, 'could sit down like the lady of Inverleith. She would sail like a ship from Tarshish, gorgeous in velvet or rustling in silk, and done up in all the accompaniments of fan, ear-rings, and finger-rings, falling sleeves, scent bottle, embroidered bag, hoop and train - all superb, yet all in purest taste; and managing all this seemingly heavy rigging with as much ease as a full-blown swan does its plumage, she would take possession of the centre of a large sofa, and at the same moment, without the slightest visible exertion, would cover the whole of it with her bravery, the graceful folds seeming to lay themselves over it like summer waves. The descent from her carriage too, where she sat like a nautilus in its shell, was a display which no one in these days could accomplish or even fancy. The mulberry coloured coach, spacious but apparently not too large for what it carried - though she alone was in it; the handsome jolly coachman and his splendid hammercloth loaded with lace; the two respectful liveried footmen, one on each side of the richly carpeted step; these were lost sight of amidst the slow majesty with which the lady came down, and touched the earth. She presided, in this imperial style, over her son's excellent dinners, with great sense and spirit, almost to the very last day of a prolonged life.'

Her son, for all the excellence of his dinners, is described by Grant as 'a man of inordinate vanity and family pride.' 'On one occasion', he records, 'when riding in the vicinity, he took his horse along the footpath, and while doing so, met a plain-looking old gentleman, who firmly declined to make way for him; on this Rocheid ordered him imperiously to stand aside. The pedestrian declined, saying that the other had no right whatever to ride upon the footpath. "Do you know whom you are speaking to?" demanded the horseman in a high tone. "I do not", was the quiet response. "Then know that I am James Rocheid, Esquire of Inverleith, and a trustee upon this road! Who are you, fellow?"

"I am George, Duke of Montagu", replied the other, upon which the haughty Mr Rocheid took to the main road, after making a very awkward apology to the duke ...'

Of Mrs Rocheid Grant concedes that her 'stateliness was not unmixed with a certain motherly kindness and

The north front of Inverleith House in The Royal Botanic Garden.

racy homeliness, peculiar to great Scottish dames of the old school.' Her imperious son, the 'eminent agriculturist', died in Inverleith House in 1824 when the villas of Inverleith Row were built on part of his property.

The mulberry coloured coach entered and left the Rocheid policies by way of Stockbridge, the entrance drive being now in the public domain as Arboretum Avenue. On the right-hand side Inverleith South Lodge is still there, along with the gate-piers surmounted by curious, old weather-beaten stone lions said to have come from Edinburgh Castle.

Of all the 'surprising quantity of architecture' in The Royal Botanic Garden the earliest and most interesting is James Rocheid's Inverleith House itself, the architect, in 1774, being David Henderson. It stands on a hill commanding an unrivaled view of the city skyline towards which it presents a tall and austerely Georgian garden frontage of three storeys and an attic above a half-sunk basement. To the north this 'plain, douce Laird's mansion' (*Edinburgh: An Illustrated Architectural Guide* 1982) has a rounded projecting stairtower behind a porch, ornamented with urns, which was added at a later date.

In 1863 this house and its immediate environs became the last residence of the Scottish antiquary and historian Cosmo Innes (1798 - 1874). A native of Deeside, he came to Edinburgh to attend the High School and subsequently went on to the universities of Aberdeen, Glasgow and Oxford. In 1822 he became an advocate at the Scottish bar. His practice was never large but the interests to which he later devoted his life were foreshadowed in his frequent employment in peerage and other legal cases requiring historical and genealogical research. Appointed Sheriff of Moray in 1840, he resigned twelve years afterwards to take up the office of Principal Clerk of Session in Edinburgh. His knowledge and understanding of the old Scottish records were revealed in his editorship of the Bannatyne, Spalding and Maitland Clubs of all of which he was an active member. He was also a prolific writer and among his publications were, in 1860, *Scotland in the Middle Ages* and, a year later, *Sketches of Early Scotch History*. According to R.G. Cant, the author of *A Short History of the University of St Andrews*, the 'task of investigating, examining and editing' the records of Glasgow University was 'brilliantly accomplished by Cosmo Innes.' From 1846 until his death he held the position of Professor of Constitutional Law and History at Edinburgh University.

Married, in 1826, and the father of nine children (his eldest daughter Katherine becoming, in 1855, the second wife of the celebrated Scottish bibliophile and historian John Hill Burton), Innes died suddenly at Killin, while on a tour of the Highlands, on 31st July 1874. He was buried in Warriston Cemetery on August 5th.

As already mentioned, fourteen acres of Rocheid land

had been acquired by the Edinburgh Town Council in 1820 and to this area the old physic gardens were then removed, the laborious task taking almost three years to complete. The transference of trees proved particularly difficult. In the Tropical Palm House, and now nearly two hundred years old, is a West Indian fan palm which was among those which were brought from the Haddington Place Garden. On the death of Cosmo Innes his ground at Inverleith was bought by the city and incorporated in the Garden. As well as greenhouses and hothouses, a museum, a library, a herbarium and an aquarium were then provided for the use of students. In 1877 what Grant calls 'a public arboretum' of about thirty acres to the immediate west of the Garden was purchased, £18,408 being contributed towards the cost by the city and £16,000 by the Government. Inverleith House then became a finely situated official residence for the Regius Keepers who were invariably also professors of Medicine and Botany at the University of Edinburgh. They delivered their lectures in the class-room in the Garden. The arboretum was to be placed 'under the Public Parks Regulations Act of 1872' and was to be maintained by the Government. In addition, 'the trustees of both Sir William Fettes and Mr Rocheid were bound to provide proper access by good roads and avenues to the ground and to give access by the private avenue leading from St Bernard's Row to Inverleith House' - the latter being the original Stockbridge entrance drive, with lodge and lion-topped gate-piers, of the Rocheids. The purchase price of the house itself was £4950.

In 1814 a gardener called William M'Nab had been appointed Curator of the Leith Walk Garden and it was his son, James M'Nab (1814 - 78), who was given a similar appointment in the Inverleith Garden by the Edinburgh surgeon Dr John Hutton Balfour, Regius Keeper for thirty-four years until his retirement in 1879. James M'Nab remained Curator till his death. Experimental

Gardens extending to ten acres were added during his curatorship and planted with conifers and evergreens, and a rockery (which was replaced by the present Rock Garden during the years immediately preceding the First World War, thus bringing its size to nearly two acres) was constructed for the cultivation of alpine and dwarf herbaceous plants. He was 'one of the original members of the Botanical Society of Edinburgh, founded in 1836, and in 1872 was elected President, a position rarely, if ever, held by a practical gardener.'

In 1887 the Cockburn Association suggested the provision of a gate from Inverleith Place into the Arboretum (now much smaller than it was originally but then a separate, western extension of the Garden, when the combined area was known as The Royal Botanic Garden and Arboretum, which was entered from Arboretum Place) 'as a boon to the public'. 'The Board of Works', to quote Rosaline Masson again, 'saw no objection to the gate if the Fettes Trustees would provide an entrance from Inverleith Place.' So the Cockburn 'presented a largely signed Memorial to the Trustees' and then complained a year later that the 'work of laying out the Arboretum has not of late been forwarded with the energy which the City has a right to expect.' There had, however, they were told, 'been no annual grant in the Estimates of the present year, and the charge of the Arboretum has not been handed over to the Botanic Garden Authorities.' To this the Cockburn responded diplomatically, declaring that 'the Arboretum with its splendid trees and beautiful views will undoubtedly become one of the most favourite resorts in the City and should be made as accessible and convenient as possible for all who may expect to frequent it, either for study or recreation.'

The following year the Cockburn Council recorded its satisfaction that 'arrangements have at last been completed for opening the gate between the Arboretum and the Botanic Gardens' and the author goes on to ask 'Who

in Edinburgh today [1926] does not know the Arboretum
and the pleasant walk right through it and on to the
Botanic Gardens?' As far as gates from Inverleith Place
are concerned, there are in fact two at the present day—
one immediately west of No. 39 and a larger entrance
(no longer in use) further west.

But as the nineteenth century drew to a close a greater
difficulty lay ahead. 'In July 1896 the Fettes Governors
proposed feuing the ground near the Arboretum. This
meant high tenements, shutting out the view of Edinburgh. The Cockburn approached the Governors, and
asked for concessions—restrictions on the height of the
buildings, or otherwise. The Governors held that they
could not, for the sake of the public good, risk pecuniary
loss; but they agreed to postpone the date of their sale,
and gave the town the option of purchase.

The Cockburn utilised the postponement of date to
some purpose. They tried the Town Council and tried the
Fettes Trustees, they personally conducted tours to admire
the view, and they aroused interest individually. It was a
story of energy, diplomacy, bluff and beneficence. The
end was success. The Lord Provost and magistrates acquired the ground for £10,000 and the view was saved.'

The Cockburn Association had also reacted with indig-
nation 'when the trees that formed the avenue to
Inverleith House suffered damage from "hordes of boys",
and some branches were "actually hacked off by an axe".'

'The modern development of the Garden' (*The Royal
Botanic Garden—The Garden Companion*) 'may be said
to have begun in 1888 when Sir Isaac Bayley Balfour was
appointed Regius Keeper of the Garden, and when soon
thereafter the Garden came under the control of Her
Majesty's Office of Works' (which became the Department of the Environment). This development was
continued by his successor, Sir William Wright Smith,
who enlarged 'the vast Rock Garden' constructed by his
predecessor and laid out the Heath and Peat Gardens. A

new glasshouse range and new accommodation and equipment for botanical teaching and research (which, along with 'that branch of botany known as taxonomy, which comprises the accurate identification of plants and their classification', has always been the principal *raison d'être* for the existence of the Garden) was the work of Bayley Balfour. For the furtherence of these aims, the Herbarium, which is considered as the main centre outside China for the study of Chinese plants, houses a vast collection of specimens, and the Library is one of the richest taxonomic libraries in the world. Under one roof, and by the architect Robert Saddler of the Department of the Environment, both were opened in 1964. With its white walls and large, prominently arcaded windows, this building together with the large Lecture Theatre entered from Inverleith Row is an outstanding landmark well beyond the Garden itself.

Among the glasshouses (all part of the 'surprising quantity of architecture') great interest attaches to the Old Palm House (or Old Palm Stove—the Tropical House). Small and octagonal, it dates from 1834, when Professor Robert Graham was Regius Keeper, cost around £1,500, and has 'splendid cast-iron spiral staircases set into the stone buttresses' (*Edinburgh: An Illustrated Architectural Guide*, 1982). Outgrowing the house, several palms succeeded in sending their leaves through the roof to a considerable height. The New Palm House (or Temperate Palm House) alongside it, built in 1858, was designed in rectangular form by Robert Matheson and cost £6,500. Towards the cost of the Temperate Palm House Professor John Hutton Balfour was successful in persuading Parliament to vote £6,000, augmenting his arguments with photographs showing several palm trees projecting many feet above the Old Palm House roof! With its wall-pilasters dividing the tall, round-headed windows, the New Palm House might be mistaken, were it not for the soaring glass roof (at a height of 70 feet 6

inches it is the tallest glasshouse in Britain), for an eighteenth century orangery. Most of the plants were
contained in tubs until shortly after 1890 when they were
replanted directly in the ground. Robert Matheson (1808
- 77) was also responsible for the class-room and earlier
museum of 1850. Immediately north of the Herbarium
and Library is the Laboratory block by W.T. Oldrieve,
of 1909, fronting Inverleith Row.

A group of Monkey Puzzle trees (*Araucaria araucana*)
stands leftwards of the main approach to the glasshouses.
These well-known conifers were introduced into cultivation in 1795 by a former pupil of Professor John Hope
of the Leith Walk Garden called Archibald Menzies who
brought back four specimens from an expedition to Chile.
The discovery in South Patagonia of great quantities of
petrified araucarian cones believed to be as old as seventy
million years bears witness to this tree being a long-stand-
ing native of the regions around southern America. A few
other trees too tender to survive out of doors are grown
in the Temperate House.

In 1965 the New Glass Houses were constructed to an
innovative design, consisting of interior and exterior
frames, the former being glazed, held together by tension
cables, by George A.H. Pearce and John Johnson of the
Department of the Environment. Really a series of connected planthouses, for which the top soil was brought
from an area around the Forth Road Bridge during road
construction work, they constitute *The Glasshouse Experience*, each house resembling a wild habitat with
temperature and humidity which change perceptibly as the
visitor explores them along the lay-out of paths and
walkways. The Fern House (with its Tree Ferns and
Giant Horsetails) is at the west end of the range, with
the Orchid and Cycad House behind the Tropical Aquatic
House in which, in summer, can be seen the Amazonian
waterlily (*Victoria amazonica*) whose huge round leaves
with upturned edges expand at the rate of a square foot

a day in the height of summer. Also situated here is the Exhibition Hall commemorating the services to The Royal Botanic Garden of the Regius Keepers and Curators from 1670 to 1970 while, resited in April 1993 beside the West Gate, the Garden Shop was originally here as well. This complex of buildings is located in the north-east corner of the Garden.

Lying in the Fossil Garden on the west side of the glasshouses is The Craigleith Tree, the long fossilised trunk of the primitive Gymnosperm *Pitys Withami* which was discovered by Henry Witham in Craigleith Quarry in 1830. An explanatory inscription gives its age as over 300 million years and states that the coal-like fragments on the trunk are probably the remains of bark. Behind the tree are the fossilised cast of the roots of a giant clubmoss (*Stigmaria Ficoides*) and an inscription which records that it 'lived in the great coal-forming forests of the Carboniferous period (350 - 280 million years ago).'

Opened in 1740, Craigleith Quarry was owned by the

The ancient Craigleith Tree in The Royal Botanic Garden before removal to its present site in the Fossil Garden.

Rocheids of Inverleith. During the construction of the National Monument stone was brought to the Calton Hill from this quarry which thereby gained an interesting reputation. As the lintel of the unfinished structure measured 130 feet in length, was 20 feet square and weighed 15,000 tons, Craigleith has the distinction of having yielded the largest single stone obtained from any British quarry.

Near the Rock Garden to the south-east of the Botanic Garden can be found the Caledonian Hall, the former hall of The Royal Caledonian Horticultural Society. Used by them as their Exhibition Hall, it later became, from 1890 until 1964, the original Herbarium. The architect, in 1842, was David Cousin (1808 - 78), who played so large a part in the laying out of the Garden Cemeteries. Of Victorian cottage design, it is noteworthy for its beautifully worked floral bargeboarding at the eaves.

With the founding of The Royal Horticultural Society in 1809 we again encounter the irrepressible Patrick Neill of Canonmills. Active in the varied fields of printing, scientific and literary work, gardening and the planning of cemeteries, he was certainly no slouch which no doubt explains why, like King Charles's head, he keeps reap-

The Caledonian Hall in The Royal Botanic Garden during 'The Botanic Ash' Exhibition in 1993.

pearing in the history of this area. One of the main instigators who, under Dr Andrew Duncan, obtained the required royal charter for the setting up of the Society, it was he who designed the ten-acre Experimental Gardens which were amalgamated with The Royal Botanic Garden when the Government acquired the property of the Horticultural Society.

On a pedestal inside the entrance to the Caledonian Hall stands a bust of Dr Neill by William Steele commissioned by The Royal Horticultural Society to commemorate 'its founding member.' The wall-mounted inscription goes on to state that 'Patrick Neill was a master printer and publisher based at Canonmills in North Edinburgh. He was also a man of science with a passionate interest in gardening. Neil was responsible for

Dr Patrick Neill from the book *The House of Neill* commemorating the bicentenary of Neill & Co, the famous Edinburgh printers. (Photograph courtesy The Royal Botanic Garden Edinburgh)

both the draining of the Nor' Loch which formerly lay in the shadow of Edinburgh Castle and for the planning and laying-out of the renowned Princes Street Gardens that took its place. The Society awards a medal in his honour for meritorious contributions to horticulture; similarly the Royal Society of Edinburgh awards the Neill Prize for achievements in Natural History.'

The Hall is now used for a range of relevant exhibitions and in 1993 an exhibition of particular relevance to the evolution of The Royal Botanic Garden itself drew many people to see the story of *The Botanic Ash*. This tree, of the British native species *Fraxinus excelsior*, was planted around 1820 and it stood, at the foot of the hill overlooking the Peat Garden, for about 170 years. As this was the year in which the Garden began its transference from Leith Walk to Inverleith, its active life covers the entire history of the Garden at its current location.

The ash tree had a height of nearly 25 metres and was 15 metres wide and, apart from releasing oxygen and water, it produced 1.6 kilograms of sugar per hour. However, as it had become ravaged and weakened by basal rot caused by fungus, it was deemed to be unsafe and was felled in November 1992 and taken to the Edinburgh District Council's sawmill at Inverleith.

The bark of the ash was then acquired by the sculptor Tim Stead who carved the wood sculptures which were the main subject of the exhibition. Having trained as a sculptor, he became addicted to wood from which, working in the Scottish Borders, he creates wood sculptures and furniture in which the form and character of the wood are allowed to dictate the size and shape of the finished work. His most famous production is the throne used by Pope John Paul at Murrayfield during his visit to Edinburgh in 1982.

Ground for a Demonstration Garden, which is still in use, was a rather later acquisition at the extreme northern edge of the 'Botanics' on the south side of Inverleith

Place. A hedge separates the Demonstration Garden from the Herbaceous Border and the Cryptogamic Garden lies to its immediate west. The study of non-flowering plants (which were given the blanket name of Cryptogamia by the great Linnaeus himself), such as ferns, mosses and fungi, and their apparent lack of any means of reproduction, had been of interest to Dr John Hope in his work at the Haddington Place Garden. As a result of his teaching on this subject one of his pupils was later to make advances in this field by his discovery, through microscopic observation, of the germination of fern spores.

One of the most attractive features of the Garden is the Pond which lies a short distance north-west of the entrance gate at the top of the approach avenue from Inverleith Row. This small, crescent-moon-shaped lake, its flat little boat usually moored mid-pond when not in use, was created out of a bog after the Garden had been relocated in Inverleith in 1820. Fed by land drains, the water supply is constantly maintained even during periods of prolonged drought. Now carried up to the Rock Garden by means of a pump, the water is led back by a recently constructed series of cascades down which it descends before re-entering the Pond.

Among the large number of plants in the Pond are the native yellow water lily (*Nuphar lutea*), Bulrushes (*Typha*) and Cape Pond Weed (*Aponogeton distachyus*) with its white flowers floating on the surface of the water during summer and autumn. The large-leaved, rhubarb-like *Gunnera manicata* from South Brazil is conspicuous among the marginal vegetation, while early spring colour is produced by the Golden weeping willow whose long yellow shoots are at their best in March.

The boggy nature of the ground in this area is especially noticeable after rain when much of the Pond Lawn takes on the characteristics of a marsh.

The Garden produces a magnificent display of colour throughout the flowering season. Particularly impressive

The Pond in The Royal Botanic Garden in 1993.

are the Azaleas, and also the many varieties of Rhododendron which have been made the subject of specialist
research. Education plays a large part in the Garden's
work programme with courses available each year to
schools from northern England and the whole of Scotland
as well as adult groups.

The Woodland Garden, which has been described as
an oasis where moisture-loving rhododendrons and even
temperate rainforest trees thrive out-doors, lies to the
west of the Rock Garden. On top of The Hill, golden
with daffodils in spring, south of Inverleith House is a
view indicator giving the names of natural features and
prominent buildings on the horizon from the Calton Hill
with its monuments to a fold of the Pentland Hills. The
boards which used to stand by the path southwards of
The Pond with names and illustrations of the different
birds which can be found in the Garden were removed
some years ago.

In 1960 the interior of Inverleith House was adapted to a new and much more public role when the old Rocheid mansion became the Scottish National Gallery of Modern Art, a function it continued to serve for twenty-five years. Throughout these years many special exhibitions were mounted (especially during the Edinburgh International Festival) in addition to the permanent display of the Gallery's own collection. The decision to use the lawn on the south side of the house as an open-air sculpture gallery was an inspired one and several examples of the work of Henry Moore became familiar to those who make regular visits to the Garden, in other parts of which works by the sculptress Barbara Hepworth have also been displayed. The name of Henry Moore has been indirectly associated with the Garden since 1961 when an exhibition entitled *Henry Moore 1928 - 1961* was presented by the Gallery. One of his last works, *Reclining Figure: Hand, 1979*, made at the age of eighty-one, has recently been placed in the care of the Garden, on loan, by the Henry Moore Sculpture Trust. Works by Barbara Hepworth, Andy Goldsworthy and others form a small collection of out-door exhibits at the Garden to which additions may be made from time to time.

Although the Modern Art Gallery was removed to the former John Watson's School in Belford Road in 1984, exhibitions, usually of botanical subjects, and, indeed, on the subject of the Garden itself, continue to be held in the rooms previously occupied by the canvases of Impressionist and later artists.

But the architecture has not been exhausted yet. The lodge at the West Gate in Arboretum Place, once the Rocheid gardener's cottage, has been altered to contain the Garden Shop which was moved here, as already noted, in April 1993 and in which, for the first time in the history of the Garden, plants are now sold to the general public. In 1989 the B-listed stables of Inverleith

House were converted into the Terrace Café, designed by the Property Services Agency and costing £340,000, as the previous tearoom was proving too small and as the provision of more ambitious facilities was considered necessary—for the Garden staff as well as for visitors. It takes full advantage of the panoramic view from its situation on The Hill.

The Inverleith Garden is augmented by three Specialist Gardens in different parts of Scotland. The first of these, gifted to The Royal Botanic Garden in 1929, is the Younger Botanic Garden at Benmore near Dunoon. Here over 250 species of rhododendron, and conifers which include some of the largest in the British Isles, form outstanding collections. Then, in 1969, came the Logan Botanic Garden near Stranraer in south-west Scotland. All but surrounded by sea and warmed by the Gulf Stream, exotic plants, including Tree Ferns and Palms, thrive beside herbaceous plants and unusual flowering shrubs from the Southern Hemisphere in the mild climate of this interesting garden. The most recent acquisition, Dawyck Botanic Garden south-west of Peebles, became part of The Royal Botanic Garden in 1978 and is renowned for its collection of magnificent trees. Daffodils followed by rhododendrons in spring, and maple and beech trees in autumn, fill the woodland walks, where there is also abundant wildlife, with photogenic colour.

The Edinburgh Garden received its royal status in 1699 and the office of Regius Keeper is therefore a Crown appointment. In recent years the Regius Keepers have included:

Isaac Bayley Balfour: 1882 - 1922
William Wright Smith: 1922 - 1956
Harold Fletcher: 1956 - 1970
Douglas Henderson: 1970 - 1987
David Ingram: 1990 -

On the wall outside the Tropical Plant House is a plaque which commemorates 'Sir Isaac Bayley Balfour Keeper of these Gardens 1888 - 1922, and is set here by his colleagues and friends to record the zeal with which he worked and the affection which they bore him.' Born in 1853, he was the son of John Hutton Balfour, Professor of Botany in the University of Edinburgh. After qualifying, he spent some time in Glasgow, and also in Oxford where he was Professor of Botany and where he carried out a number of improvements in the Botanic Garden. Later, in Edinburgh, he was prominent among those who prevented the Inverleith Garden from passing into the hands of the University. He died in 1922.

The present Keeper is the fourteenth holder of the office and already he has become involved in new projects such as the setting up of the Botanics Trading Company and the Friends of the Royal Botanic Garden. International collaborations have been launched and twinning has taken place between the Edinburgh Garden and The Kunming Institute of Botany in Yunnan in China.

In 1993 The Royal Botanic Garden became the first botanic garden to win the Royal Horticultural Society's Rothschild Challenge Cup for a display of rhododendrons. It was also the first time that this award had come to Scotland.

The Botanical Society of Edinburgh, which was founded on 8 February 1836 at No. 15 Dundas Street where a carved tablet records the event, was based at the Inverleith Garden. Now the Botanical Society of Scotland, its function is to promote the study of plants and to exchange botanical information between members. It is still based at The Royal Botanic Garden in Edinburgh with which it has close links, as it has also with the botany departments of Scottish universities, and regular meetings are held at the Society's branches in Glasgow, Aberdeen, Dundee, St Andrews and Inverness. It publishes a scientific journal, *The Botanical Journal of Scotland*, and a regular newsletter.

The Linnaeus Monument in The Royal Botanic Garden stood originally in the older Garden at the top of Leith Walk.

Each year, in December, an exhibition is held at the
Garden on the subject of *A Garden in the Desert*. Two
plants which figure in this exhibition are myrrh and
frankincense, so familiar from the Biblical accounts of the
Nativity of Jesus but about which so little is otherwise
known. The resin from the bark of both plants was expensive and highly regarded in ancient times and they
grew, as they still do, in India, Arabia and Africa. Frankincense is of particular interest in this Scottish Garden
because of its botanical name, *Boswellia*, which commemorates Dr John Boswell, the uncle of the more famous
James, the biographer of Dr Samuel Johnson.

The Inverleith Garden is Scotland's own national Botanic
Garden as well as an international scientific research institution specialising in plant taxonomy. It was administered by
a Board of Trustees and funded by the Department of Ag-

riculture and Fisheries for Scotland until becoming a non-departmental public body, with charitable status, in 1986.

The 'Botanics' are in the forefront of British initiatives to save the plants and animals of the world and of research into sustainable systems of land management and halting the destruction of the rainforests. In 1991 the Edinburgh Centre for Tropical Forestry was set up as a joint venture by the University's School of Forestry, the Institute of Terrestrial Ecology, the International Forest Science Consultancy and The Royal Botanic Garden which, in the same year, set up at the Inverleith Garden a Rainforest House as part of its *Living in a Rainforest* exhibition. The house, in addition to being the centrepiece of the exhibition, was also used as a classroom for a schools programme. The Exhibition Notes draw attention to the 'humid, dense and verdant tropical rainforests' which are 'the richest source of life on the planet—home to over half the wild animal and plant species in existence.' 'Somewhere between destruction and preservation there is a sustainable and sensitive alternative for managing the resources of the rainforest.'

Information available at *The Glasshouse Experience* explains that 'For over 300 years the Garden has been concerned with the exploration of the Plant Life of our planet' and one of its most important aims is to provide 'an understanding of the ecology and distribution of plants, thus defining how they grow and the impact of global warming, acid rain or other pollution on their status—knowledge that is fundamental to the vital task of conserving the plant communities on which everyone's future ultimately depends.'

In enjoying the peace and beauty of Inverleith's Royal Botanic Garden, which is visited by over three-quarters of a million people every year and is one of Scotland's principal tourist attractions, it should never be forgotten that it plays so large and so important a part in the

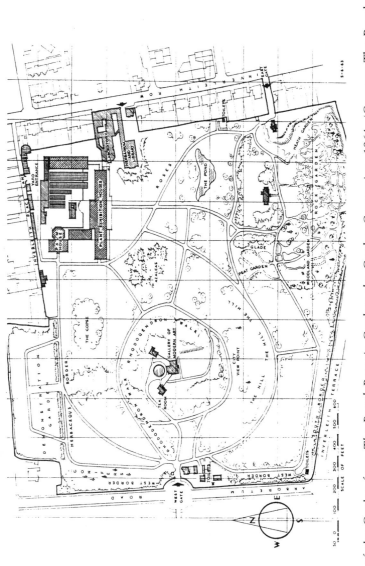

Plan of the Garden from *The Royal Botanic Garden: the Garden Companion*, 1964. (Courtesy The Royal Botanic Garden Edinburgh)

world-wide effort, against daunting odds, to save the environment for future generations.

CHAPTER 10

Inverleith Row and Inverleith Place

Building in Inverleith Row, in front of The Royal Botanic Garden, began in 1823 (although No. 1a and the terraced houses Nos. 1 - 4 by David MacGibbon were as late as 1862) and the row of villas on the western side is described as 'an outstanding series' in *The Buildings of Scotland: Edinburgh*. Each villa had to have a minimum cost of £500 and was given gardens to the front and rear. No. 8, on the north side of the entrance to the Botanic Garden, was the work of the New Town architect, W.H. Playfair (1790 - 1857) for his own relative Daniel Ellis, a military surgeon. In 1923 this house was donated to Broughton Place (later Broughton McDonald and now Broughton St Mary's) Parish Church as a manse and it continued to be so used for exactly fifty years when a smaller house was purchased by the church.

Some Edinburgh citizens of note have kept house in Inverleith Row. Among them was Thomas Chalmers (1780 - 1847), his name inseparable from the Disruption in the annals of Scotland, who lived at No. 7 before the building, in 1842, of his house Churchhill (later renamed Westgate House), the first one to be built in Churchhill Place.

Dr Chalmers was born in Anstruther, where his father was a dyer and shipowner, and in 1791 became a student of both Arts and Divinity in the United College of St Salvator and St Leonard at St Andrews University when just eleven years of age. He went on to lecture in Mathematics there before going to Glasgow where he spent some time. Returning, however, to St Andrews in 1823 as Professor of Moral Philosophy, his strong revulsion against a number of abuses at the University was soon leading him into vehement criticism of such malpractices

as 'the Candlemas Dividend', as it had come to be
known, whereby the professors of the United College
were wont to augment their own emoluments by sharing
out among themselves the annual surplus revenues of the
college! Thomas Chalmers was ordained a minister in
1803 and, after the Disruption, became Principal of the
Free Church College in 1845, two years before his death,
worn out by his many exertions, at Churchhill. He was
buried in the Grange Cemetery where the monument
erected to his memory can still be seen.

At No. 15 Inverleith Row lived Eve Blantyre Simpson,
daughter of Sir James Young Simpson who, like Dr Chalmers, died from physical exhaustion in middle life. Next
door to each other stayed the families of the Edinburgh
jewellers and silversmiths, still well known today, Messrs.
Hamilton and Inches, the Hamiltons at No. 17, which is
now an Abbeyfield House, and the Inches at No. 18.
Founded in 1866 by Sir Robert Kirk Inches, Lord Provost
of Edinburgh between 1912 and 1916, the firm moved
from No. 88 Princes Street to No. 87 George Street after
the Second World War and was bought in April 1992
by the Bond Street jewellers the Asprey Group. It holds
a Royal Warrant as silversmiths and clock specialists to
Her Majesty the Queen.

The artist William Hole (whose mural paintings in the
former St James' Church are described in Chapter 13)
lived at No. 27 in the 1890s before his removal to 13
Inverleith Terrace. No. 29 was the home of the Edinburgh writer and historian Moray McLaren and his wife,
the actress Lennox Milne, while the late Sir Thomas Innes
of Learney, a former Lord Lyon King-of-Arms, resided at
No. 35.

Inverleith Nurseries lay in the gap between Nos. 47
and 50 Inverleith Row, a gap which has in recent years
been closed with the building of flats.

Continuing northwards, and still on the west side of
the street, No. 52 constitutes a link between Inverleith

and the Napoleonic Wars. It was here that the veteran soldier, Lieut.-General William Crockat, spent the last tranquil years of his long and eventful life. In 1807, says James Grant, whose industrious research brought to light this information, 'he was gazetted an ensign in the 20th Regiment of Foot', and went on thereafter to distinguished military service at the battles of Vimiera, Corruna and Vittoria in Spain. The French Wars at an end, he accompanied his regiment to the island prison of Napoleon Bonaparte where he was the last officer to take charge of the 'caged eagle of St Helena' who died there under his guardianship. Captain Crockat, as he was at that time, was then sent home to announce the news. After spending the rest of his active life in India, he retired to Edinburgh where, 'in spite of war, wounds and fever', he lived for nearly fifty years before his death, in 1874, in his villa at Inverleith Row, 'a hale old relic of other times'.

No. 52 was the residence of The Right Hon. Sir Louis S. Gumley while Lord Provost of the city in 1938.

On the east side, Eildon Street is reached immediately north of Lothian Regional Council's Warriston Private Playing Fields (whose red sandstone gate-piers front Inverleith Row at its junction with Howard Place) over which it looks towards Warriston Crescent. This street owes its name to Alexander Henderson, a former owner of the lands of Warriston, who lived in Eildon Hall beside the Eildon Hills in Roxburghshire. It starts at the Inverleith Row end with tenements but continues gently downhill to the east with terraced houses (many now subdivided) of 1879 (Nos. 1 -18) and then of 1906, these having interesting Edwardian coloured glazing (which it has been made obligatory to replace if broken) in the upper part of the windows. No doubt this site, once part of the old (West) Warriston House estate, was acquired to provide its residents with the open, panoramic view of Arthur's Seat and the Old Town skyline which, with the city street-lights and the floodlighting of the Castle, becomes spectacular at night.

The twentieth century enclave of Eildon Terrace, Warriston Drive, Warriston Gardens and short adjacent streets lies beyond Eildon Street to the north, as also does Warriston Cottage, No. 101. The oldest house in Inverleith Row, it grew to its present size after being disjoined from the Warriston House estate on which it probably served as a gardener's but-and-ben cottage in the eighteenth century. The remains of a curved garden wall were found near the cottage. In the 1930s it was in the possession of Thomas Methven & Sons whose seed warehouse was at No. 113 George Street and whose Warriston Nurseries were here. The white-washed, two-storey house it has now become stands, looking north and south, behind a wall and is again in residential occupation.

In a straight line from the west side of Inverleith Row to East Fettes Avenue, and crossed midway by the junction of Arboretum Road and Arboretum Place, runs the part-Georgian, part-late Victorian Inverleith Place. The Georgian houses, all c.1825 and each costing a minimum of £1,000, have Doric entrance porches, No. 39 having been designed by Thomas Brown (c.1781 - 1850), the architect of the former St Mary's Church in Bellevue Crescent. To the immediate south of this and the adjoining houses on the east side can be seen from Inverleith Place the two Palm Houses of The Royal Botanic Garden.

Randall Thomas Davidson (1848 - 1930), of the family which gave its name to Davidson's Mains, was born at No. 15 Inverleith Place. He was appointed Domestic Chaplain to Queen Victoria in 1878 and, as Archbishop of Canterbury from 1903 - 28, he crowned King George V in 1911.

No. 37 has an unusual history. Once the Scottish home of the kings of Norway, it became, in the 1950s and '60s, an electronics medical research centre where such inventions as the foetal heart monitor were worked out. The owners were Bruce Peebles & Co. Ltd. of East Pilton, then one of the biggest industrial concerns in the city, who had been suppliers of material for military use during the Second World War and who had applied to the Edinburgh Corporation Planning Committee for permission to use No. 37 Inverleith Place (a house which has seen many alterations and additions) as an electronics laboratory. Satisfactory sound-proofing was a condition of the Corporation's agreement, as was the maintenance of a residential appearance of both the house and garden. A large part of the villa was occupied as offices, while the remainder became laboratory workshops with small machine tools and electronic apparatus. This house is now the School of Post-Graduate Studies of the Edinburgh College of Art.

No. 48 Inverleith Place, the home of Col. and Mrs McFeat and the 'bronze cockerel'.

The large late Victorian villas lie further west, one of the most notable being the half-timbered, Tudor-style No. 48 by Stewart Henbest Capper (1859 - 1924), better known for his work in the Royal Mile for Patrick Geddes than for villa building though he also designed Edzell Lodge, No. 34 Inverleith Terrace. Both of these Henbest Capper houses were built in 1895.

It was in this elegant family house that the saga of the 'bronze cockerel' was brought, after many vicissitudes, to its fitting conclusion. This statuesque bird, two feet, six inches in height and weighing about a hundredweight, was in 1915 found in the First-World-War-devastated town of Ypres by the late Colonel Peter D. McFeat, then a young lieutenant in the Royal Engineers, while clearing a path for his lorry through scattered bricks and rubble immediately after the Second Battle of Ypres. Pierced by shrapnel and with a shattered base, it had escaped neither unscathed nor unnoticed, for Lieut. McFeat rescued the damaged bird and from then until the last years of his life it travelled with him, like a treasured trophy, around the world. This prolonged itinerary started with twenty years in China, where the colonel was a coal mine administrator and where a new base was made for it by an Italian sculptor, and was followed by locations, during and after the Second World War, which included Africa, Burma, India and even Siberia. Its wanderings at last behind it, the cockerel was allowed to fold its wings for a time in the quiet and dignified surroundings of Inverleith Place, No. 48 being the home of Col. McFeat and his wife, Maude, in 1956.

At the age of ninety-two the colonel, deciding that 'it was time the bird flew home', wrote to the Belgian Embassy in Edinburgh where arrangements were made with the commander of a flotilla of Belgian ships then docked at Leith for its final journey. Lt.-Commander Xavier Coucke of the *Zinnia*, the flotilla's flagship, declared himself 'honoured to take the bird home' where it is now

Col. and Mrs McFeat handing over the 'bronze cockerel' to Lt. Commander Coucke of the Belgian Navy at 48 Inverleith Place. (Photograph courtesy The Scotsman Publications Ltd)

one of the principal exhibits at the First World War Museum at Ypres. So, after sixty-six years, the much-travelled cockerel returned to base on the 24th of July 1981. The type of building—some mansionhouse, perhaps, or possibly a farm—on which it had once been an ornamental feature will probably never be known; but the building had been in Ypres—that much was certain. Col. McFeat, C.B.E., who had been awarded the Military Cross among other campaign medals, remembered for the rest of his life the smell of gas at Ypres and the 'hellfire' at the Menin Gate. 'I'm glad to see the bird fly home', he said.

Ecton Lodge, No. 32 Inverleith Place, was built in 1900 and is noteworthy, with its obelisk finials and its leaded windows, for its English Jacobean style.

North of Inverleith Place and branching westwards from Arboretum Road is Kinnear Road (called after Lord Kinnear, a Trustee and Governor of the Fettes Trust) in which, erected beside the Edinburgh Academy New Field, are three Edinburgh Academy boarding-houses, Jeffrey House, Scott House and Mackenzie House. The first two were built in 1899 and Mackenzie House, by Ramsay R. Traquair, son of the painter Phoebe Traquair and architect of the former Christian Science Church in Inverleith Terrace, dates from 1910. The two playing fields of the Edinburgh Academy, the Sports Ground and the New Field, are situated to the south and north respectively of Inverleith Park. The houses in Inverleith Avenue South date from the early twentieth century. This short street is closed off at the north end by a private entrance to the Royal Botanic Garden across which rises the tower of Inverleith Parish Church.

Returning to the northern section of Inverleith Row, Warriston Nurseries, now built over, lay to the immediate north of Warriston House at the end of the nineteenth century, and north of the Warriston Nurseries the widespread Bangholm Nursery extended north to, and to the north of, Ferry Road and east to the Edinburgh, Leith and Granton branch railway line. Part of this land was used for tenement building off Inverleith Row and part became the Sports Ground of George Heriot's School.

CHAPTER 11

Inverleith Park

Separated by Arboretum Place, which runs between them, Inverleith Park lies to the west of The Royal Botanic Garden. The east gate is a memorial to Alison Hay Dunlop and has rusticated piers supporting lions, while that to the north, dated 1891, is in the form of a pedimented arch. The architect of both gates was Sydney Mitchell. The Park stretches from Inverleith Place on the north to the back of the Edinburgh Academy Sports Ground and the Grange Cricket Ground on the south, and is bounded on the west by East Fettes Avenue. The Grange Cricket Club celebrated its 150th anniversary here at Raeburn Place in 1982 with a dinner held within Fettes College, a school which has provided them over the years with many talented players.

Laid out by Edinburgh Corporation in 1890, Inverleith Park is divided into four quarters by two paths. Where the paths intersect stands a fountain within a rough, unhewn granite obelisk designed by William Hole in memory of John Charles Dunlop (d. 1899), a magistrate of the city (he had been elected a Councillor for St Bernard's Ward) and the brother of Alison Hay Dunlop whose book *Anent Old Edinburgh* was published, after her death, in 1890 and was the first book borrowed (by the Earl of Rosebery when he opened it) from the Carnegie Free Library, now the Edinburgh Central Public Library, in George IV Bridge. She and her brother collaborated in the production of an earlier volume which is still of great interest. This was *The Book of Old Edinburgh and Hand-Book to the Old Edinburgh Street, For the International Exhibition of Industry, Science and Art, Edinburgh 1886, with Historical Accounts of the Build-*

Alison Hay Dunlop, author of *Anent Old Edinburgh*, who is commemorated by the east gate at Inverleith Park.

ings therein reproduced and Anecdotes of Edinburgh Life in the Olden Time, illustrated by William Hole, A.R.S.A.

Set out across The Meadows, this was the first international Exhibition to be held in Scotland and among those who donated items for the construction of the Old Edinburgh Street were James Ballantine & Son, already mentioned in connection with Warriston Cemetery, who provided 'Ancient stained glass.' John Charles Dunlop, whose bronze portrait medallion by George Webster on the fountain was obliterated by vandals many years ago, was Joint Convener of the 'Old Edinburgh' committee for the setting up of the Exhibition. He had been one of the principal movers for the creation of the Park and the fountain was erected by public subscription in 1900.

The east gate is opposite the west end of Inverleith Terrace and the path from the entrance leads to the former farmhouse of Inverleith, or South Inverleith, Mains, the old home farm of the Rocheid mansion. It was built during the eighteenth century but was altered and modernised in 1900, this date being clearly visible above the door. A porch, probably an earlier entrance, can be seen at the other side of the red-roofed building which has tall chimney stacks above the gables. An ancient bow, or archery, butt, the last surviving remnant of the old castle or fortalice of Inverleith (Grant records 'archery butts, 600 feet apart, standing nearly due south of Inverleith Mains'), was sited to the south-west of the farmhouse and is shown on a Post Office Directory map of 1914 as lying to the west of Portgower Place. This map also shows, within the Park, the Pond and the 'Pavilion

The former Inverleith Mains Farmhouse in Inverleith Park.

Gardens' on the north side of which is indicated a 'Pavilion'. This is now the Sundial Garden where a sundial is inscribed *Presented by Councillor Kinloch Anderson, 1890. The Buildings of Scotland: Edinburgh* refers to 'a serpentine path with a pond and small formal garden' on the south side of the Park which can be entered, near the Pond, at the north end of Portgower Place, the southern approach to this much-used and much-appreciated open space within the city.

Inverleith Pond lies towards the south-west corner and its banks, in the early years of the Park's existence, were regularly taken over as a drying and bleaching green by the local citizens. The bank sloping southwards towards the sun was the bleaching area, while poles and clothes ropes were provided for hanging up the remainder of the washing. In 1947 the pond was drained for the first time in twenty-three years and in 1959 the bottom was covered with special gravel to restrict the growth of weed which impeded the sailing of model yachts and other small craft. Being up to four or five feet deep in places, it was considered dangerous for young children and to remedy this the city's Parks Department, after consultation with model yachting enthusiasts, dumped tonnes of broken rocks and similar material on the pond bed so that it is now just over two feet deep overall.

In 1966 the Inverleith Model Yachting Club was given permission to use the Pond on one Sunday each month during the season and in September 1981 the first Scottish Model Yacht Racing Championship was held, the boats, costing about £100 and weighing around 15lbs, were required to have a sail area not exceeding 800 square inches. Club racing continues throughout the winter. The Pond is used for skating and the measures taken to regulate the depth have been beneficial to the skaters also. It is now drained annually to clear out accumulated rubbish.

This shallow pleasure-pond, straight along its southern side and gently rounded towards the north, is home to a number of swans and ducks but even here, in what might be thought a reasonably safe environment, they have been subjected to the vandalism which is now endemic in society. As recently as 17 December 1990 oil drums, or used fuel canisters, were thrown into the water. Eight swans and some ducks were affected and it took several weeks to clean and medicate the birds.

After the accession to the throne of Edward VII in 1901, his coronation was celebrated by a Sports Day in Inverleith Park when 'various wards in the city competed in the races and St Bernard's Ward did particularly well on that occasion' (*Stockbridge House—The Project* by Una Maclean and Harry Rankin).

In a letter to an Edinburgh newspaper a few years ago the correspondent recalled Inverleith Park 'in the years before the fateful month of August 1914, when the part now occupied by allotments was then an excellent 19-hole pitch-and-putt course. There was also an excellent "Ride" reserved for the use of those who loved horse-riding.' The Ride consisted of a long, straight avenue between trees on the north side of the Park.

An attempt was made in 1984 to use part of the Park as an open-air sculpture gallery, a venture which had proved highly successful in the neighbouring Royal Botanic Garden, but vandalism put a stop to this as well. Nine giant works by the Edinburgh sculptor Adam Zyw went on show in the Sundial Garden at the end of June with the intention that they would remain there until the end of September. But they had to be removed a few weeks earlier because of deliberate damage. The first attack took place shortly after the exhibition was opened, when a steel figure was found to have been bent, and the sculptor had then to spend, in his own words, 'more time mending stuff than getting on with new work.'

The imaginative suggestion was made, in 1992, that the so-called Trinity College Apse in Chalmers Close between the High Street and Market Street, all that remains of the medieval Trinity College Church which was removed from its original site to accommodate the tracks and platforms of the Waverley Station, should be rebuilt in Inverleith Park to become The National Gallery of Scottish Art. Here, it was proposed, would be exhibited, along with many other paintings from Scotland's heritage, the four surviving panels of the Trinity College Altarpiece by Hugo van der Goes which were part of the furnishings of the church and which are presently displayed in the National Gallery of Scotland. This intriguing possibility was the brain-child of the Edinburgh District Council, but no decision has yet been made. Another suggestion was that it be rebuilt in the grounds of the former Dean Orphanage at Belford.

In May 1993 the Scottish International Children's Festival, the largest arts festival for the young in the United Kingdom, was held in Inverleith Park.

CHAPTER 12

West Inverleith

Running west from the north end of Inverleith Row, on the line of Ferry Road and opposite the south end of Wardie and Granton Roads, is Inverleith Gardens. Here, consisting of Nos. 22 and 23, is a 'twin late-Georgian villa', as it is described in *The Buildings of Scotland: Edinburgh*, easily discernible by its plain but symmetrical architectural style in comparison with its Victorian neighbours of the 1880s. It must have stood here, in comparative isolation, for thirty or forty years before the rest of the street was built.

At the east end, No. 1 Inverleith Gardens, before and after the Second World War, was occupied by the Stafford House China Store prior to its removal to Tollcross, and Blanche & Co., the Grocers and Italian Warehousemen, had their shop at No. 8 around 1890. Further west stands Inverleith Parish Church and manse.

The first Free Church of Scotland place of worship for the residents of Granton and Wardie was an iron church at the foot of Granton Road capable of seating a congregation of four hundred, which was in place just six weeks after it had been ordered from a London supplier in 1874. Known as Granton and Wardie Free Church, it had cost £625. The district was then very sparsely populated but that situation was about to change and by 1878 the possibility of building a larger and more permanent church was already being discussed, and, indeed, in the following year a hall was erected in Bayton Terrace for work among the young. (Before it was fully built, part of Granton Road was known as Bayton Terrace.) When an offer of £25 per acre for a site at the north end of Wardie Road was rejected as insufficient by the owner, General Boswall (who would not agree to less than £60), the feuing of ground in Inverleith Gardens facing the top of Granton Road was then successfully pursued and the firm of Hardy & Wight, who carried out a large amount of church building in Edinburgh, was asked to draw up plans. This time the cost was £5,000 which was raised from a Free Church grant, a bank loan, a two-day bazaar in the Music Hall in George Street that realised the very considerable sum, at that time, of £1118, and the sale of the iron church to Berwick-upon-Tweed Congregationalists at Spittal for £325. It was opened on 3rd June 1881 under the new name of St James Free Church and the same architects were called

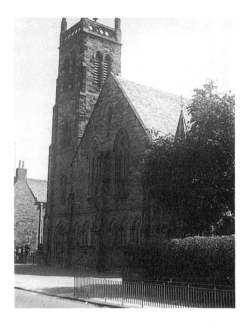

Inverleith Parish Church at the top of Granton Road.

back three years later to design a hall at the south-east end of the building at a further cost of £437.

In 1899 one of its most able ministers, The Rev. Thomas L. Ritchie, was inducted to the charge and it was during the first year of his ministry that the amalgamation of the Free Church and the United Presbyterian Church (the famous U.P. kirks of Stevenson's poem) took place in 1900 when another change of name was required, this time to St James United Free Church. Mr Ritchie, whose health was impaired by many difficulties during the war years of 1914 - 18, died in 1919 when his place was taken by The Rev. Arthur Cowan. Increases in activity and membership necessitated the building of a new Session Room, which could be used as an addition to the Church Hall, in 1925 when kitchen and other facilities were also provided. Four years later, in 1929, the last of the great Presbyterian reunions, that between the United Free Church and the Church of Scotland, took place, when the church became, and has since remained, Inverleith Parish Church.

A year later the church building was seriously damaged by a fire which broke out in the early hours of 10 December 1930. Offers of help were immediate. The neighbouring church of St Serf's opened its doors to the Inverleith congregation whose Kirk Session recommended the building of a temporary hall for use while repairs were being carried out. But this proved to be unnecessary when an invitation from the Rector of the Edinburgh Academy to hold services in their hall was gratefully accepted. For a year, the time required to complete the work of restoration, members were taken to the hall each week in three buses. The organ had been totally destroyed and a decision was made to relocate the new instrument in the front of the church instead of in the gallery. All was finished early in 1932 when, on the 23rd of February, the reconstructed and redecorated building was rededicated along with a new pulpit incorporating a baptismal font.

Notwithstanding these problems, Inverleith Parish Church played a vital role during the years of the Depression in the 1930s, Dr Cowan becoming president of the Leith Unemployed Men's Club, set up in 1932, when funds for the club, and also for the provision of Sunday services for the unemployed in the old Alhambra Theatre in Leith Walk, were provided by the church.

Throughout this period the development of the surrounding district was continuing and a new hall, known as the Large Hall, was built (at a cost of £3,000) and opened on 17 December 1937, the year in which Dr Cowan attained his golden jubilee in the ministry, thirty-seven of those years having been devoted to the Inverleith congregation. His death took place, unexpectedly and while on holiday, in 1959.

The centenary celebrations of the church in 1981 included, most appropriately, a fête in the Edinburgh Academy Preparatory School in Arboretum Road, a centenary concert by the Edinburgh Academy choir and orchestra and the puplication of a book, *Inverleith Church 1881 - 1981*, by Alexander Fraser.

The church building, Gothic Revival in style and cruciform in plan, dominates the view southwards up Granton Road with a massive gabled frontage. Adjoining this on the eastern side rises a tall tower terminating in four pinnacles and containing in its base the arched entrance to the vestibule above which the gallery, the location of the original organ, is situated. A bell was installed in the tower in 1961. On the western side of the church stands the manse, also by Hardy & Wight and built, at the same time as the church, in 1881. Incorporating several styles of architecture, it repeats some of the features on the church exterior and is entered by a projecting porch. When it was occupied by the first minister, The Rev. Peter C. Purves, it was called Cheviot Cottage and appears to have been owned by him as *The Kirks of Edinburgh 1560 - 1984* states that it was purchased

from his widow by the church in 1919. It was not unusual, in the Secession and Free churches, for the minister
to live in his own house.

Next to the manse is Rosetta, a large villa which was
designed by Robert R. Raeburn, the architect of Ashbrook further west in Ferry Road, in 1880 and which
gives Inverleith its second link with the Emperor Napoleon and his *grande armée*. It was called, by William
Wishart, an early owner who had had business interests
in Egypt, after the famous Rosetta Stone which provided
the key to an understanding of Egyptian hieroglyphics.
On this block of granite is engraved a public notice in
three languages, one of which, being Greek, enabled the
other two (the picture language known as hieroglyphics
and a simpler type of writing called demotic script) to
be deciphered. A French officer of Napoleon's Engineering
Corps discovered it in 1799 half buried in mud at the
mouth of the Nile near Rosetta, not far from Alexandria,
when the French Expeditionary Force was fighting the
Turks at Aboukir. After the British Army had captured
Alexandria and defeated the French in 1801 they brought
the stone back with them to England and it is now in
the British Museum in London. William Wishart owned
the house from the 1890s till his death but it remained
in the possession of either his daughter or his sister until
1916. The stables were converted to a garage in the
twentieth century.

There is at least one other house, although it is not
in Edinburgh, called after the Rosetta Stone. In 1807
Thomas Young, a Scottish army surgeon who had served
in Egypt during the campaign, bought a small estate just
outside Peebles called Acrefield on which he built a large
house for himself and, on his marriage shortly afterwards,
his wife. The old name was immediately abandoned,
when the estate and the small mansionhouse became
known as Rosetta. It subsequently gave its name to Rosetta Road in Peebles and, now incorporated within the

town, still stands today. The interesting story of the house and its builder is given in *Thomas Young of Rosetta*, a booklet, published in 1980, which is available at the John Buchan Centre in the village of Broughton.

On the west side of Rosetta is Inverard which was the home, until about 1940, of William Duncan of Duncan's Chocolate Factory at Beaverhall Road. It is now a home for the elderly and includes several small individual houses built within the garden ground as well as Inverard itself.

Beyond Inverleith Gardens, on the north side of Ferry Road, was the farm of Windlestrawlee, so called from the crested dogtail grass known as windlestrae, a name which, in Scotland, was also used for moorland grass and bent. The farmhouse has survived the inevitable changes here. No more than a single-storeyed, whitewashed cot-

The Ferryfield Gates in Ferry Road.

tage which was extended to provide a byre, the two parts are easily distinguishable by the windows and a chimney in the cottage and the skylights in the byre roof. For many years the green turf of the former farmland, bounded on the east by Boswall Drive, served as the sports ground of Melville College and later, after their amalgamation, of Daniel Stewarts Melville College, the Ferryfield gates having been presented by former Melville College pupils at the club centenary in 1965. The exceptionally fine playing fields covering seven acres at the east end of the ground then belonging to the Edinburgh Merchant Company (of whose four schools Daniel Stewarts (now Stewarts Melville) is one) were sold in 1981 and are now the site of a residential development called Ferryfield built shortly afterwards.

The original Stewart's College Sports Ground lies on the opposite (south) side of Ferry Road on the former farmland of North Inverleith Mains (also known as Blaw Wearie). This is now the Stewarts Melville Sports Ground. Further west was the farm of East Pilton.

To the west of Inverleith Park beyond East Fettes Avenue, and with a sports ground which stretches behind it up to Ferry Road, stands the 'Scottish baronial-French Gothic masterpiece of David Bryce' (*The Buildings of Scotland: Edinburgh*), Fettes College, completed in 1870 on the Comely Bank estate of Sir William Fettes whose bequest financed the cost of its construction. Described in Peter Williamson's Directory of Edinburgh as 'William Fettes, grocer, head of Bailie Fife's Close' in the High Street, he was twice Lord Provost of the city in the opening years of the nineteenth century. The College (which became co-educational in 1981), being within the district of Comely Bank, cannot be claimed as more than a dominant landmark in Inverleith, but Sir William Fettes (1750 - 1836) has a closer connection as he has given his name not only to East Fettes Avenue but also to Fettes Row which terminates the northern New Town above Canonmills. He started, at the age of eighteen, as a wine and tea merchant and went on to become a maritime under- writer and to develop connections with the British Linen Bank. Knighted in 1804, he bought several estates, includ- ing Comely Bank and Gogarbank, and lived at No. 11 Charlotte Square.

Carrington Road, to the west of East Fettes Avenue, is called after the politician (and later Governor of New South Wales), the third Lord Carrington who was a Gov- ernor of Fettes College, the grounds of which are bounded on the south by Carrington Road. The first three Fettes boarding-houses, Moredun (built 1870), Car- rington (1872) and Glencorse (1873) (all in an anglicised baronial style) are within the College grounds, the first two fronting Carrington Road and the third East Fettes Avenue. A fourth boarding-house, Kimmerghame, was built in 1928 between Carrington House and Crewe Road, the western College boundary. In 1988 thirteen acres of Fettes land were sold for £2.8 million and this sum has been used to finance major refurbishment at each of the boarding-houses. Fettes Village, a development which includes houses and leisure facilities, has been laid out on this site.

On the north side of Ferry Road between Ferryfield on the east and the recently-built residential area called Winnelstrae on the west stand two houses—Ashbrook and Wardieburn House—which juxtapose diametrical extremes of architectural dissimilarity, the former an essay in Ital- ianate Victoriana, the latter high-piled and baronially Scottish. The sombre-looking Ashbrook, by the same ar- chitect, Robert R. Raeburn, as Rosetta in Inverleith Gardens, was built in 1869 and has a low tower crown- ing the two storeys with arcaded windows underneath. It was the home of Sir Robert Maule, proprietor of Maule's, a department store at the west end of Princes Street which is better known at the present day as Binns and then as Fraser's.

In 1872 Robert Maule and his son removed to Leith from their native Kincardine-on-Forth where the elder Maule had been in business as a draper and general furnisher for some years. The Popular House, his Leith emporium, was in Tolbooth Wynd and he advertised regularly in *The Leith Burghs Pilot* offering such bargains as 'pure coloured silks' at 1/6d (8p) per yard and 'Real Brussel carpets' at 2/8d (14p) per yard and delivering in Leith and district every hour! The store was transferred to Princes Street in 1893. Sir Robert retired to The Lea in Corstorphine, in which house he died, aged 69, in 1926 when he was described as a generous benefactor and a respected citizen in *The Edinburgh and Leith Observer*.

Firmly in the Scottish vernacular tradition, Wardieburn House rears its crow-stepped gables and asymmetrical windows to third floor level where a gabled, tower-like feature contains a single central window at the same height as the chimney-stacks. Built at much the same time as Ashbrook, it has belonged to the bakers, D.S. Crawford Ltd., for many years. The original Wardieburn House, after its demolition, was replaced on the same site by the Northern General Hospital (built in Ferry Road in 1893 as the Leith Public Health Hospital) and Wardieburn Road and its adjacent streets between Boswall Parkway and Granton Crescent were built, in 1932 - 3, on the west side of the now culverted Wardie Burn flowing from the vicinity of the Hospital to Granton Harbour.

CHAPTER 13

Goldenacre

At the north end of Inverleith Row the area of the old Wardie Muir, or Moor (across which Ferry Road was built in the eighteenth century to provide a link between Leith and South Queensferry), is reached. It was created by the melting of the ice (by which the land had been depressed during the Ice Age) and the consequent considerable rising of the ground to form a raised beach which slopes steeply down to the present sea level, as can be clearly seen in several streets in Trinity. The moorland soil was unsuitable for the growing of crops with the exception of that part which has for long been known as Goldenacre but which was originally called Goldenriggs where the ripening corn turned the fields to gold at harvest time. Strictly speaking, the name applies only to the eastern side where the land was owned by the Dukes of Buccleuch, the 5th Duke (who was also the 7th Duke of Queensberry—1806 - 84) having been responsible for the construction, at his own expense, of Granton Harbour in the 1830s. Through this harbour esparto grass was imported for the paper mills of the Lothians, many of them powered by the hard-working Water of Leith. Goldenacre is on the road from Leith to Granton.

Some of the streets here owe their names to the Buccleuch connection. Granton itself means The Farm by the Shore and is first mentioned, as Grantaine Cragg, in 1544 when Hertford's army disembarked there before marching across the Muir to a skirmish at Puddocky Ford. But Montagu Terrace, Royston Terrace and, eastwards round the Ferry Road corner, Bowhill and Monmouth Terraces are all of Buccleuch derivation. The house called Royston Mains (probably, in view of the word 'Mains', a farmhouse) was on the site now occupied by No. 231 Granton Road.

Bowhill, in Selkirkshire, is one of the residences of the Dukes of Buccleuch.

In 1767 Henry, the third Duke, married Lady Elizabeth Montagu, the only daughter of George, 4th Earl of Cardigan and afterwards Duke of Montagu, and the Dukes of Buccleuch themselves are descended from James, Duke of Monmouth, an illegitimate son of Charles II who put himself at the head of a rebellion for which he was subsequently executed by his uncle, James VII and II. Royston, however, can be traced to a much nearer source. It was taken from Granton Castle, once known as Royston Castle, which became Buccleuch property by inheritance in 1794.

A large part of the original Goldenriggs became the Bangholm Nursery in the nineteenth century and extended north across Ferry Road to the rear of the demolished Bangholm House (Bangholm Bower House off South Trinity Road is still, though now sub-divided, in existence) and south to the Warriston Nurseries on the north side of Warriston House in Inverleith Row. Part of the Bangholm Nursery is now the Sports Ground of George Heriot's School, the Sports Ground being confined to the south side of Ferry Road. Murrayfield Rugby Ground replaced its predecessor here at Goldenacre in 1925, in which year the Heriot grandstand, with its somewhat unsightly back to Inverleith Row, was built.

The little hamlet of Bangholm consisted of a small community with cottages and a smithy and the streets, built in 1924 - 5, of Bangholm Grove, Loan, Park, Place, Road, View and Villas are on the site of Bangholm Farm. Bangholm Terrace is earlier in date and was built, off Inverleith Row, on Bangholm Nursery ground, as were the parallel Goldenacre and Royston Terraces. Bangholm Bower Avenue is the original driveway to the house of Bangholm Bower to the north of Ferry Road in Trinity.

On the west side of Inverleith Row to the north of Inverleith Place was the extensive Inverleith Nursery, with nursery ground spreading westwards as far as East Fettes Avenue before streets and playing fields were laid out across it. All this nursery ground, providing a livelihood for market gardeners, was between Ferry Road on the north and Inverleith Park and The Royal Botanic Garden on the south, and here they tended the vast stocks of shrubs, fruit trees and ornamental plants for which they were famed within the city. More recently, a newspaper report in 1957 stated that 'not many yards from Goldenacre, but unsuspected even by local residents, a mink farm was run by a Polish ex-Serviceman.'

On the eastern Goldenacre corner are four-storey flats, with shops beneath, built in 1879, and McVitties, Guest & Co. Ltd. occupied Nos. 1 and 2 Bowhill Terrace for many years before and after the Second World War. On the western corner Inverleith Row terminates with another late nineteenth century tenement block above ground-floor shops.

The most significant building—and it is of great interest—in Goldenacre is the Scottish Episcopal Church of St James the Less, now known as St Philip's and St James', on the west side of Inverleith Row. This congregation, however, has its roots in the eastern New Town rather than in Inverleith. It was in 1821 that the block of tenements on the corner of Broughton Street and Broughton Place was built, betraying no sign of the church which had been incorporated within its walls, even the windows differing not at all from those of the surrounding flats. Occupying the first floor and containing two galleries, it could accommodate a congregation of eight hundred. These premises were acquired some considerable time ago by the Jehovah's Witnesses and are now in use as a Kingdom Hall, the adjoining St James' Church School, which appears originally to have had a connecting door into the church, being still in place and recently occupied as an Edinburgh Unemployed Workers Centre.

In 1883 the Broughton church was sold for £1250 and ground for a new church building in Inverleith, where many members of the congregation were now resident, was feued from the Fettes College Trustees. To begin with a Hall only, costing £799, was built and in it the congregation worshipped for the first five years after which it became, and is still today, the Church Hall. A competition was, however, held to obtain a suitable design for a church and this was won by the outstanding Scottish architect Sir Robert Rowand Anderson (1834 - 1921) (who had already designed the former Catholic Apostolic Church at East London Street) whose completed red sandstone building, in fourteenth century Gothic style on its somewhat restricted site, was opened for worship in 1888, the last Rector of 'Old' St James' and the first of 'New' St James' being The Rev. Jacob Simmins. His successor was The Rev. Charles J. Jenkins who served in that office from 1892 until his untimely death in 1917. (Notwithstanding that Rowand Anderson was a member of St Cuthbert's Church, Colinton, his funeral was held from St James' in Goldenacre.)

The east gable of the chancel, with its large, five-light window with curvilinear tracery, faces the street and an extension adjoining (which now has a pyramidal roof) on the southern side was intended, in accordance with the architect's original plan, to have supported a steeple rising to a height of 110 feet and a bell tower but these were not, as had been hoped, subsequently built. Two of the five intended bays were also omitted. The cost of the church, minus these features, was £3,500.

The great glory of this church is undoubtedly the interior where the work of the artist William Hole, R.S.A. (1846 - 1917) has recently been restored. William Hole, born in Salisbury and a member of the St James' congregation, lived at No. 27 Inverleith Row in 1896 and in 1916 at No. 13 Inverleith Terrace. The work with which his name is most usually associated is in the

Edinburgh City Chambers where, between 1903 and 1909, he executed the wall paintings of Scottish historical subjects in the Dining Room (now known as the European Room). The frescoes in St James' were slightly earlier in date, being carried out 'as a labour of love', as Gilbert Cole records in *A Church in Goldenacre*, during the years 1892 to 1902, and it was as a direct result of his work in St James' that he was commissioned to execute the City Chambers decoration. The frieze of celebrities from Scottish history in the entrance hall of the National Portrait Gallery in Queen Street was also designed by him during its construction in the late 1880s.

Taking the *Te Deum Laudamus* as his principal theme in St James', the artist covered the chancel walls with depictions of prophets, apostles and martyrs above vines and peacocks (the latter symbols of immortality) in a dado at a lower level. A procession of over thirty life-size figures, their faces turned towards the altar, progresses across a central panel. The Holy Church is represented by bishops from Africa, a priest and a deacon, a friar and a nun—symbolising catholicity—and for them contemporary divines, including the then Rector of St James' The Rev. C. J. Jenkins, were used as models.

In all this work a large amount of gold was introduced, the gilding itself being done by David Dall, verger of the church for thirty-four years, who brought to the task his expertise as a house-painter. William Hole also carried out the stencilled fleur-de-lys and monogram motifs on the nave walls, the nave being united with the chancel by a lettered *Te Deum* frieze. Among the figures on the north wall is the patron saint of the church, St James the Less, carrying in his hand a small model of the church. These spirit frescoes (being carried out on dry rather than the more usual wet plaster) are now in the care of the Department of the Environment.

The tile and marble chancel was the work of Sir John J. Burnet, R.S.A. (who commenced the refurnishing of the

St James' Episcopal Church in Inverleith Row. (Photograph courtesy Mr Gilbert Cole from his book *A Church in Goldenacre*)

interior in 1894 and who was asked to produce a chancel design worthy of the frescoes of William Hole) in 1902. The choir stalls and altar rail, in Japanese oak, were also executed to his designs, while the segmentally-pedimented triptych, above the altar and in the Pre-Raphaelite style, is by William Hole. At the west end of the south aisle is the Baptistry (also by Burnet) and it is through its traceried screen that the nave is entered. The stained-glass windows here were the work of Douglas Strachan and the figure of the Good Shepherd and the white marble font are by C. d'O Pilkington Jackson. The spacious nave has an open kingpost roof and, on the centre pier, a beautifully carved Madonna and Child which, together with a wooden Crucifix which is now in the Christ

Chapel, came from St Aidan's Church, Niddrie Mains. The pulpit is a memorial to The Rev. Jacob Simmins.

The first radical change since the removal from Broughton took place when a link was established between the congregation at Goldenacre and that of Christ Church in Trinity Road. This resulted in the closure of Christ Church in November 1980 when the congregations united to become Christ-Church-St James', all services being held in the Goldenacre building.

The beautiful, small Episcopal church on the corner of Trinity and Primrose Bank Roads had been built, as a private chapel, in 1854 in the Middle or Decorated Gothic style, its spire rising beside the west gable into the surrounding trees. Of the two church buildings 'St James' is Edwardian, large and richly decorated', as Gordon Donaldson has written, 'whilst the smaller Christ Church is Victorian with the simplicity of a village church.' It was built and owned by The Rev. Walter Goalen of Starbank House in Trinity and he was the sole incumbent until 1875, in which year it was purchased by the congregation (and became part of the Scottish Episcopal Church) to serve residents in Trinity and North Edinburgh. The church was enlarged in 1889 by the addition of a north aisle containing fifty-six sittings. There had only been accommodation for 148 and additional pews were required when sailors and marines from naval gunboats and cutters lying in Granton Harbour during the winter months started attending its services on a regular basis. The War Memorial was by Sir Robert Lorimer in 1921 and the history of the church was written by the late Professor Gordon Donaldson, Historiographer Royal in Scotland, at the time of the centenary in 1954. He tells of a dispute between the members and one of the Rectors which resulted in a number of families leaving to join 'a new congregation worshipping in a mission Chapel at the head of Inverleith Row'—the infant St James' at Goldenacre. And he also records 'the most strenuous objection' which had been made by members of the Christ Church vestry when the St James' mission chapel had been opened! All this had been long forgotten by the time persistent financial difficulties at Christ Church necessitated the union with St James' when the little church was sold for £31,000 and converted, some of the stained-glass being retained, into a dwellinghouse.

Many of the furnishings of the former Christ Church were preserved, including, among other items, the original stone altar, two stained glass panels and a silver alms dish. At the instigation of the Rector, The Rev. (later Canon) Rodney Grant, a disused cloakroom to the rear of the nave and opposite the Baptistry was transformed into the Christ Church Chapel and here the cherished artefacts from the Trinity church are now displayed.

The Rev. Charles Jenkins had started a mission in a hall in Beaverbank Place in Canonmills to provide an outreach by St James' into the wider community, the hall being furnished, and equipped with everything from cups to cupboards, by generous gifts both from the members of St James' and the local residents. The hall was officially opened at an evening service on 11 January 1895 and, in addition to services, the premises were kept in constant use by such other activities as concerts, lectures and a Working Men's Club. Among those who took part in them was William Hole, the artist of the St James' frescoes, who was, says Mr Cole, 'an accomplished actor and elocutionist.'

The Canonmills mission was so successful (as early as 1896 the Sunday School was attended by eighty children) that a fund was started for the building of a church to replace the rented Beaverbank accommodation. Sir John Burnet, who had already carried out extensive work within St James' at Goldenacre, was chosen as the architect, and St Philip's Church in Logie Green Road at its junction with Broughton Road was duly opened by the Bishop of Edinburgh, The Rt. Rev. Dr John Dowden, on

12 June 1908. Constructed in red brick 'except for the harled and cottage-windowed nave which is built on top of the arched and massively buttressed hall' (*The Buildings of Scotland: Edinburgh*) and with a red brick interior, a porch and vestry were added in 1922 and a reredos depicting the Tree of Life by the sculptor A. Carrick Whalen was placed in the Children's Chapel in 1950.

A suggestion in the early 1970s that St Philip's, which was giving active and ongoing help to the many families in the Canonmills area which were, to quote Mr Cole again, 'often in dire need', might be able to become an independent church was not found to be a viable possibility, but all indecision about its role was resolved when it was linked, under a scheme involving team ministry in north-east Edinburgh, with St Margaret's, Easter Road. This led to the founding of the Canonmills Community Care organisation, an arrangement which made maximum use of one of St Philip's greatest assets, its spacious premises in Logie Green Road.

Especial concern was felt for the young unemployed, and it was therefore with a real sense of achievement that, with the support of the Manpower Services Commission, the Canonmills Community Care YOP scheme was set up in 1982, a scheme which was run successfully for a number of years. But financial problems were being experienced by St Philip's to such an extent that the closure of the church became a matter of urgent consideration. In 1986, however, this dilemma was overcome when The Rev. Rodney Grant accepted a proposal by The Rt. Rev. Richard Holloway, the Bishop of Edinburgh, that, while St Margaret's should unite with Old St Paul's in Jeffrey Street, St Philip's should be similarly attached to Christ-Church-St James', thus bringing it back, so to speak, to its mother church which had launched the Canonmills mission in 1895.

These developments entailed a change of name for the third time at the former St James' at Goldenacre and it now became St Philip's and St James', the Christ Church connection being enshrined in the Christ Church Chapel in the Goldenacre church which continues to be used for the combined congregation, as do the church premises in Logie Green Road as well, 'in the building up of life, worship and community service.' The present Rectory is in Wardie Road.

When a new organ was installed at the back of the nave in the Goldenacre church in 1982 the opportunity was taken to create a more convenient entrance to the church in place of the original doorway in the south-west tower over which it had been intended to build a spire. A new door was opened, much closer to the street, leading into the former organ chamber where the open arches into the church were then filled in. In addition the rood beam which had been designed by Sir John Burnet as a memorial to The Rev. Charles Jenkins and placed at the entrance to the chancel in 1922, was removed to the new vestibule. Gilbert Bayes, the London sculptor, had designed the five figures, coloured to harmonise with the frescoes, mounted on the beam.

By 1985 alarming structural problems had developed which necessitated the vacation of the Goldenacre church for a period of ten months, a sum of nearly £60,000 being donated by the Historic Buildings Council towards the cost of their repair. To quote from a short Guide to the church prepared during the following year, 'the sleeper walls upon which joists and flooring are laid collapsed or subsided, taking flooring with them and twisting pews and stalls', the collapse being due to traffic vibration and the settlement of the walls themselves. This situation was now remedied, in Gilbert Cole's words, by abandoning 'the old sleeper walls and beams', constructing 'a "raft" of solid steel girders' and laying down 'a new hardwood floor', the only measures which could be adopted 'if St James' was to be saved.' Canon Grant (who has since retired) and the congregation worked tirelessly to raise their share of the increasingly large expenditure required and 'a piece of unwanted land to the rear of the church' was sold as a housebuilding plot, thus adding well over £27,000 to the Reconstruction Fund. 'In the end the total bill came to £65 short of £120,000'. But on Sunday, 22nd June 1986, when the praise was accompanied 'by the brilliant sound of the Monktonhall Colliery Silver Band', 'the congregation was back in church at last!' So St Philip's and St James' now faces the future, at Goldenacre and Canonmills, and its continuing task of Christian work and witness, with renewed confidence and hope and in the knowledge that they have a secure base from which to go out into the community.

Fourteen years before Jules Verne wrote his classic book *Around the World in Eighty Days* the famous French traveller had set out with a friend on a journey through England and Scotland in which, as he claimed to have Scottish ancestry, he had a particular interest. Subsequently he wrote (in the only recently published *Backwards Through Britain*) of their experiences, calling himself Jacques and his companion Jonathan. Arriving in Edinburgh by train from Liverpool in 1859, their minds filled with the novels of Sir Walter Scott and especially with *The Heart of Midlothian*, they had immediately set out to explore the Old Town, and he writes engagingly of the Canongate and the Grassmarket and Arthur's Seat, of what they admired or did not admire, and of how it was impossible to take a step in Edinburgh without encountering the living traces of Mary Queen of Scots—'in any case', said Jacques, 'she was half French. Frenchmen are bound to honour the memory of the Duke of Guise's tragic niece'—or 'stepping into one of Scott's poignant ruins.'

But they had another destination in view as well. Jonathan's brother had married the niece of a 'respected Scotsman' who lived in Inverleith 'and the young man knew he would be made very welcome if he called on the family'. Having studied a plan of the city in their hotel, they walked 'in the direction of Leith', observing that each front door in the New Town was approached over a small bridge and under a Greek portico. Jacques read out the names of the residents' professions as they walked past. Eventually they reached an elegant avenue called Inverleith Row and, half a mile down, came to 'an attractive residence, with a neat, dainty look about it, and tall windows that thirsted for daylight and fresh air. Railings enclosed a small front garden'.

When Jonathan rang, the door-bell was answered by a servant who led them up a 'gleaming staircase covered with a narrow carpet to a first-floor drawing-room' where two women, 'intent on needlework', were sitting. After the young Parisians had introduced themselves, and learned that their visit had been expected, they were soon in lively conversation, especially with the daughter of the house, Amelia, by whose courtesy and grace they were very agreeably impressed. Amelia had been well instructed in the French language and Jacques was delighted that, her Scottish accent notwithstanding, here was someone with whom he could have a 'sustained conversation' in his native tongue.

Before long a visit to the Botanic Garden, which was 'just down the road', was suggested where, as it was Saturday, the hothouse would still be open. Jacques offered Miss Amelia his arm. 'She took it graciously' and they were soon at the Garden 'with its small unassuming gate' through which they were led by Amelia to 'a large glass rotunda sheltering exotic plants'.

This delightful outing lasted about an hour and then, back in Inverleith Row, Miss Amelia guided them 'across the street to Edinburgh's new cemetery as if it was a pleasure ground and the most natural place on earth to visit'. Among the lawns and box shrub borders of Warriston Garden Cemetery the visitors found the 'tombs were a pleasure to contemplate in that cool and shaded place' and Jacques, moved by this scene of eternal peace, was grateful that she had taken them 'to this entrancing park'.

Amelia's father took them, on other occasions, on further expeditions in Edinburgh and Jacques and Jonathan enjoyed their exploration of this northern capital city. But their happiest memories were of the elegant villa and its hospitable occupants and of those moments when, pleasantly tired by a long day in the wynds and closes of the Old Town, or climbing the steep ascent to the Royal Palace on the Castle rock, they heard Amelia's father say, 'And now, gentlemen, we shall return to Inverleith Row where dinner awaits us'.

Bibliography

Some Ancient Landmarks of Midlothian, Henry M. Cadell.
The Water of Leith, ed. Stanley Jamieson, 1984.
By the Water of Leith, D.P. Thomson, 1952.
The Story of Leith, John Russell, 1922.
Traditions of Trinity and Leith, Joyce M. Wallace, 1985.
Further Traditions of Trinity and Leith, Joyce M. Wallace, 1990.
Villages of Edinburgh, Vol. I, Malcolm Cant, 1986.
The Book of the Old Edinburgh Club, Vol. 12, 1923.
Memorials of His Time, Lord Cockburn, abridged 1945.
Old and New Edinburgh, James Grant, 1880.
Traditions of Edinburgh, Robert Chambers, 1846.
Georgian Edinburgh, Ian G. Lindsay, 1948.
Random Notes and Recollections of Edinburgh, T.M. Tod, 1944.
The Kirks of Edinburgh 1560 - 1984, A. Ian Dunlop, 1989.
The Story of St Stephen's, Edinburgh 1828 - 1928, Lord Sands.
A Short History of St Mary's Parish Church, Edinburgh, John W.B. Caldwell, 1992.
Canonmills Baptist Church (leaflet) 1988.
Edinburgh: Picturesque Notes, R.L. Stevenson, 1879.
The R.L. Stevenson Originals, Eve Blantyre Simpson, 1912.
Robert Louis Stevenson, James Pope-Hennessy, 1974.
Sir James Y. Simpson, Eve Blantyre Simpson, 1896.
Edinburgh, George Scott-Moncrieff, 1947.
The Dictionary of National Biography
The Dictionary of Victorian Painters, 2nd edition, Christopher Wood, 1978.
Newspaper Cuttings, Edinburgh Room, Edinburgh Central Public Library.
The Streets of Edinburgh, published by Edinburgh Impressions, 1984.
The Writing on the Walls, Elizabeth Berry, 1990.
Discovering West Lothian, William F. Hendrie, 1986.

Master Class, Robert Scott Lauder and his Pupils, National Gallery of Scotland, exhibition publication, 1983.

Once Upon a Haugh, Juliet Rees, 1991.

History of the Barony of Broughton, John McKay, 1867.

Reminiscences of Stockbridge and Neighbourhood, Cumberland Hill, 1874.

The Colonies of Stockbridge, Rosemary Pipes, 1984.

Stockbridge House, The Project, Una Maclean and Harry Rankin, 1972.

The Buildings of Scotland: Edinburgh, 1984.

Edinburgh: An Illustrated Architectural Guide, 1982 and 1992.

A History of Edinburgh Transport, n.d.

Tanfield—Site History (leaflet) The Standard Life Assurance Co. Ltd.

The Making of Classical Edinburgh, A.J. Youngson, 1966.

Precipitous City, the Story of Literary Edinburgh, Trevor Royle, 1980.

John Hope 1725 - 1786 Scottish Botanist, A.G. Morton, 1986.

The Royal Botanic Garden, The Garden Companion, H.M. Stationery Office, 1964.

4 Gardens in One, Deni Bown, 1992.

Scotia's Darling Seat, Rosaline Masson, 1926.

Dreamthorp, Alexander Smith, with Biographical Introduction by John Hogben, 1906.

Collected Poems, Lewis Spence, 1953.

The Outlines of Mythology, Lewis Spence, 1944.

Ruins and Remains: Edinburgh's Neglected Heritage, 1985.

The Edinburgh Graveyard Guide, Michael T.R.B. Turnbull, 1991.

Inverleith Church 1881 - 1981, Alexander Fraser.

The House of Neill 1749 - 1949, ed. Moray McLaren.

The Last Picture Shows - Edinburgh, Brendon Thomas, 1984.

A Church in Goldenacre, Gilbert Cole, 1991.

The Story of Christ Church, Trinity, Gordon Donaldson, 1954.

Backwards Through Britain, Jules Verne, published in French as *Voyage à Reculons* in 1989, in English by W. & R. Chambers in 1992.

INDEX